Every Day with Jesus

SEP/OCT 2008

His Story
– *Our Story*

'What is man that you are mindful of him,
the son of man that you care for him?'

Psalm 8:4

SELWYN HUGHES

Further Study: Ian Sewter

Discussion Starters: Ian Sewter (opposite 26 October)

© CWR 2008. Dated text previously published Sep/Oct 1998 as
Every Day with Jesus, The Bigger Story by CWR.
This edition revised and updated by Mick Brooks for 2008.

CWR, Waverley Abbey House, Waverley Lane, Farnham, Surrey GU9 8EP, UK
Tel: 01252 784700 Email: mail@cwr.org.uk Registered Charity No. 294387. Registered
Limited Company No. 1990308.

Unless otherwise stated all Scripture quotations are from the Holy Bible, New
International Version. © International Bible Society.

Cover image: Getty/Photographer's Choice/Richard Drury
Quiet Time image: photocase.com
Printed in Nigeria by Academy Press Plc, Lagos.

Every Day with Jesus is available in **large print** from CWR.

A word of introduction ...

'**D**azed and confused' was the reply I received recently when I asked someone how he was feeling. 'It's as if suddenly, very suddenly, the rug has been pulled out from under my feet.' That person's entire life had been turned upside down dramatically and without warning, leaving him unable to understand his new circumstances.

Often during these stormy times, or perhaps once we have regained our equilibrium, questions come knocking at the doors of our hearts: How did that happen? *Why* did that happen? Is there a plan or purpose to life?

The question of the meaning of life has been wrestled with for as long as mankind has existed. Philosophers have debated endlessly about it. Here are some of the more recent answers that I have come across: 'The purpose of life is to end'; 'Life is a game; sometimes you win, sometimes you lose'; 'Life is not a question to be answered, but a reality to be experienced'. And so at times life can seem, as Oswald Chambers put it, 'more tragic than orderly'.

In this issue of *Every Day with Jesus*, we explore with Selwyn the plans and purposes of God. Our lives, because of Jesus, have great meaning – each of our individual 'stories' has been taken by God and woven into His great salvation story. In the Bible, we see this great storyline unfolding in which we all have a part to play.

It is my prayer that as you read and meditate on the thoughts in this devotional, you will become captivated by God's story and encouraged to trust Him even when you cannot trace Him, knowing that He is an ever-present help in times of trouble.

Sincerely yours, in His name

Mick Brooks

Mick Brooks
Consulting Editor

FOR READING & MEDITATION - JEREMIAH 29:1-14
'"For I know the plans I have for you," declares the LORD ...' (v.11)

One of the most exciting ideas I have come across in my journey through the Christian life is the thought that in every believer's life a divine story is being written. Through all the countless occurrences of our lives a guiding hand is at work, taking the raw material of life and making from it a story-line that, even though it may be hidden from us at the moment, will, when viewed from the vantage point of eternity, astonish us.

Over the next two months I hope to be able to bring home to you the realisation that if you believe in the Lord Jesus Christ and have accepted Him as your Saviour then your life is not a series of haphazard events, but a narrative. God has the ability to take everything that happens to us and make out of it a story – a story that has coherence and purpose and that fits into the bigger story He is telling. A story has a beginning, a middle and an ending. Everything in it has a point. Nothing need be irrelevant.

The writer Thornton Wilder says we should think of our lives in terms of a great landscape that extends far beyond what the eye of our experience can see. 'Who knows,' he says, 'how one experience so horrible to us can set in motion a chain of events that will bless future generations?' This is the thought that must grip us as we begin our meditations: behind the seemingly chaotic and indiscriminate events of our lives a bigger story, a *divine* story, is being written. A writer has been defined as 'someone on whom nothing is missed'. The Divine Author, I assure you, misses nothing. It was said of one short-story writer that he could make a story out of a grocery list. God can do infinitely better: He can make a story out of anything.

FURTHER STUDY

Gen. 50:15-21; Acts 2:22-24

1. What was God's purpose in Joseph's story?

2. Explain why Joseph is a type of Christ.

O Father, drive deep into my spirit the truth that nothing is being missed in my life. Everything that happens to me is being used to form a story. You turn everything into something meaningful. And I am so grateful. Amen.

More than just facts

FOR READING & MEDITATION - COLOSSIANS 3:1-17

'For you died, and your life is now hidden with Christ in God.' (v.3)

We began yesterday by affirming that in every Christian's life a divine story is being written. My dictionary defines a story as 'a piece of narrative, a tale of any length told or printed in prose or verse of actual or fictitious events'. A story consists of much more than the stringing together of certain facts. It has rhythm and movement, highs and lows, light and shade, plot and counterplot.

I can tell you about my life by giving you a list of facts, but that will not tell you the *story* of my life. It is only when those facts are fleshed out with details of the dramas that have gone on in my life – with the rhythms – that it becomes a story. Dan Allender, professor of counselling psychology at Mars Hill Graduate School illustrates the difference between a set of facts and a story in this way: 'If I say, "The king died and the queen died," then all I have are facts. But if I say, "The king died *and the queen died of grief* ..." now I have the basis of a story.'

FURTHER STUDY

John 6:5-13;
1 Cor. 12:12-27

1. How did a boy's packed lunch become part of the divine story?

2. Why are we all immensely important?

We must learn to see our lives as far more than a compilation of facts, otherwise we are in danger of regarding a person merely as a biological machine. Even in the seemingly most humdrum life a story is being created that, seen from an eternal perspective, would be breathtaking. You may think your life is boring and routine, but if you are a Christian then the sovereign God is at work, weaving every fact into a story. Don't get caught up, I beg you, with the world's ideas to such an extent that you forget, as our text for today puts it, that 'your life is now hidden with Christ in God'. Any life that is in Christ has a meaning that extends far beyond what is obvious from the happenings down here on earth.

O Father, how can I ever thank You enough for the fact that my life is hidden with Christ in You? Reveal to me day by day all the implications of this tremendous truth. Help me be fully aware of its wonder. In Christ's name I ask it. Amen.

The elements of story

WED
3 SEP

FOR READING & MEDITATION – 1 THESSALONIANS 5:12-28

'And we urge you ... be patient with everyone.' (v.14)

Today we continue thinking about what constitutes a story. When I first began my ministry of writing, I enrolled in a course for writers, one section of which dealt with the technique of short-story writing. I was told that a story should have four elements: (1) characters; (2) a plot; (3) movement; (4) dénouement. Take the first element: *characters*. A good story has many different characters – lead characters, supporting characters, antagonists, and so on. In your story and mine there is a variety of characters: friends, enemies, people who are for us and people who are against us.

My pastor used to say to me when I was a young Christian, 'Always remember that the people you relate to are part of God's purpose for your life.' Non-Christians go to their graves with their character flaws largely unaltered, but with you and me it is different. Though the finishing touches will be made when we see our Lord face to face, the major shaping of our characters takes place in the here and now. God wants to make us like Jesus, and one of the ways He goes about this is by using the people who cross our paths as tools to shape us and make us more like Christ.

The people in your life, I believe, are hand-picked by the Lord to expose your temper, pride, stubbornness – whatever your struggles and difficulties might be. And running away from them is no answer. It's not worth it because God has many more such people to replace them. Make a list of all the people with whom you find it difficult to get on and ask yourself: What is God trying to show me about myself through them? Be assured of this: the characters who appear in your story are being used by God to develop your own character.

FURTHER STUDY

Rom. 12:14-21;
Gal. 2:11-16

1. How do we become more like Christ?

2. How was Peter's fault exposed?

O Father, help me grasp the fact that relationships do not so much cause problems as reveal problems. Grant that I may not miss the lessons You are trying to teach me through the people You allow into my life. In Jesus' name. Amen.

The divine plot

FOR READING & MEDITATION   ROMANS 8:28 39

'For those God foreknew he also predestined to be conformed
to the likeness of his Son ...' (v.29)

Yesterday we said that a good story contains four elements: characters, plot, movement and dénouement. Today we look at the second of these elements: *plot*. The dictionary defines 'plot' as a 'plan of main events or topics in a play, poem, novel, etc'. I am always intrigued when occasionally (very occasionally) I read the writing of a good, clean-minded novelist who takes the raw data of existence and makes out of it a story. Storytellers who are able to devise a plot and carry one along through its various twists and turns have provided me with some satisfying reading over the years. This kind of writing is not something I am able to do. Only once in my life have I written a short story, and no publisher seemed at all interested in it!

FURTHER STUDY

Col. 1:24-27;
1 Pet. 2:13-25

1. What mystery did God plot that Paul revealed?

2. Why is becoming like Christ not an easy process?

God, as we have been saying, is in the story-telling business too. But what is His plot? John Stott expresses it like this: 'God is making human beings more human by making them more like Christ.' In the beginning God created us in His own image, which we spoiled by our sin and disobedience. Now He is busy attempting to restore that lost image.

The Living Bible brings this out most beautifully when it paraphrases our text for today in this way: 'For from the very beginning God decided that those who came to him – and all along he knew who would – should become like his Son ...' God is so excited about His Son Jesus Christ that He wants to make everyone like Him, not in appearance, of course, but in character. And He uses everything that happens to us – good, bad and indifferent – to make us more like Him. What a difference it would make if we would really get hold of the truth that God allows into our lives only what He can use.

My Father and my God, help me grasp the fact - really grasp it
- that You allow into my life only those happenings - including
trials and tribulations - that further Your intention to make me
more like Your Son. In Jesus' name. Amen.

'I'll wait until I get home'

FOR READING & MEDITATION - 1 CORINTHIANS 13:1-13

'... when perfection comes, the imperfect disappears.' (v.10)

Now we look at the third aspect of good story-telling: *movement*. This has to do with the way a story unfolds. Eugene Peterson defines Christian counselling as 'listening to someone's story and looking for the movement of God'. He makes the assumption that God is always actively doing something in a Christian's life. Yet how can we believe that, when life comes to a stop and nothing seems to be happening? And what about those times when, to use the words of Shakespeare, 'Sorrows ... come not single spies but in battalions'?

Often when I have sat with a person in whose life tragedy has occurred they have asked, 'What can God be up to in allowing this to take place?' My usual response is, 'I don't know, but whatever is happening, He is going through it with you.' The time of tragedy is not a time for speaking about the ultimate problems of the universe. It is time for the upward look and trustful silence. Not every person, of course, is strong in faith and able to praise God in the midst of trouble and believe that He is bringing about something good. Most of us perhaps, myself included, would identify with a man who once told me, 'The best I can do in times of trouble and tragedy is to demonstrate mute obedience.'

FURTHER STUDY

Job 13:15;
Rev. 21:1-7

1. How did Job express ultimate faith?

2. What is God's ultimate intention?

Certain dark problems have occurred in my own life that I have never been able fully to understand. *Some* light shines upon those problems, but no *complete* solution is to hand. However, whatever God's intention, I am told in Scripture that it is good. And I hold on to that. Enough light beats on our path for us to pick our way along it. But for the final explanation we must wait until we get home, and then our heavenly Father will explain it to us Himself.

My Father and my God, help me in those moments when I can find no answers to develop the upward look and the trustful silence - to trust You even when I cannot trace You. In Christ's name I ask it. Amen.

All's well that ends well

FOR READING & MEDITATION - 2 CORINTHIANS 4:1-18

'For our light and momentary troubles are achieving for us an eternal glory that far outweighs them all.' (v.17)

The fourth aspect of good story-telling is *dénouement* – the final resolution. Soon after it was published I read *The God of Small Things* by Arundhatiti Roy, the book which won the Booker Prize for literature in 1997. Though there are some passages in the book a Christian finds unacceptable, nevertheless I was thrilled by her wonderful use of the English language, the way in which she peeled away layer after layer of mystery, and her ability to stir emotions with words. It is indeed a masterpiece of writing. But in my opinion the beauty of the book is its *dénouement*.

After reading it I could not help but ponder the question: How will the story of my own life end? What special skill will the Divine Author apply to the final details of my personal narrative? As I mused, I remembered a quote by C.S. Lewis, which came home to me with great force: 'We ride with our backs to the engine ... we have no notion of what stage of the journey we have reached ... a story is precisely the sort of thing that cannot be understood till you have heard the whole of it.'

I do not know how God will write the final pages of my personal story, but I am sure of this: it will eclipse anything written by the greatest novelist. I trust Him to do this. And so, my friend, must you. Because your life is hidden with Christ in God, you are not just a statistic in the divorce rate, a victim of menopausal depression, an 'uneducated misfit' or a 'square peg in a round hole'; your life is a drama for which, perhaps, some of the best action and speeches are yet to be written. G.K. Chesterton said, 'You cannot finish a sum how you like, but you can finish a story how you like.' All of God's stories end well.

FURTHER STUDY

Job 42:1-16;
Rev. 22:1-5

1. How did Job's story end?

2. How will our story end?

Loving heavenly Father, help me see that though You have the ability to turn all things to good, I have some responsibility too. May I so live that nothing I do will hinder You writing the conclusion You have planned for my story. Amen.

God at work

FOR READING & MEDITATION – PHILIPPIANS 2:1-18
'... it is God who works in you to will and to act
according to his good purpose.' (v.13)

Today we continue reflecting on the fact that in every believer's life a divine story is being written. We simply have to believe this. Not to believe it means that our lives fragment into a series of random events, jerky starts and meaningless cul-de-sacs. Many of us go through times when what occurs doesn't seem to make sense. But because God is at work in our lives, we can be assured that a wonderful story is being written, in which all the puzzling parts will finally fit – everything will eventually come together.

Have we not all found that years after a perplexing event has happened, suddenly it all seems to fall into place? The realisation that God was at work dawns on us and we say to ourselves, 'Oh, so that's what *that* meant.' The Almighty is not helpless in the face of the sad and tragic things that happen to us. He is busy transforming them. And He can do this with such amazing power that sometimes we look back and imagine He was the author of the evil that became the occasion of so much good.

FURTHER STUDY

Gen. 1:1-5,
26-31; 2:7;
1 Cor. 1:26-31

1. What does God work with?

2. What is the result of His work?

This is not the first time I have used the illustration of the beautiful park and boating lake in Scarborough, Yorkshire, called The Mere. Not many who are impressed with its charm know that it was created out of a garbage heap. Originally it was one of Scarborough's refuse dumps, but with scientific thoroughness and the strictest regard for hygiene the city fathers transformed it into a thing of beauty. And if man can do that, what of God? These lines sum it up beautifully:

Deep in unfathomable mines
Of never failing skill
He treasures up His bright designs
And works His sovereign will.

Gracious Father, how can I thank You enough that Your transforming power is constantly at work in my life? Things are never static. I am following an unfolding Mind and an expanding Will. Blessed be Your name for ever. Amen.

An unfolding creation

FOR READING & MEDITATION - MATTHEW 18:1-9
'If your hand or your foot causes you to sin,
cut if off and throw it away.' (v.8)

When we begin to look at our lives as stories then everything changes. Existence is not flattened out on the graph paper of analysis but comes alive in the movements of a drama – some of which is yet to be written. Many Christians have told how the concept of their lives being a story has engaged their attention and fired their imagination in a way that nothing else has done. William Kilpatrick, a Christian psychologist, claims that 'the Christian life and the imaginative life can grow up together'.

J.R.R. Tolkien went so far as to say that a Christian could, through sanctified imagination, actually 'assist in the unfolding and enrichment of creation'. Some of the great story writers, such as George MacDonald, C.S. Lewis, G.K. Chesterton, and Dorothy Sayers, were not only wonderful writers but were, at the same time, lucid apologists for the Christian faith. They opened up worlds to us because of the world that was opened up to them as they soaked their thoughts in Holy Scripture.

Do you remember C.S. Lewis's wonderful story *The Silver Chair*? The beautiful Queen of the Underworld nearly convinces the children from the Overworld that her own dismal kingdom is the only reality, and theirs but an imagined dream. The young prince, the two children, and their companion, a Marsh-wiggle, are in danger of falling prey to the Queen's blandishments when the Marsh-wiggle, to prevent the Queen's words taking hold, thrusts his foot into the fire. The shock helps him face reality, and as he speaks up, the children see the point he is making, run to his side, and escape. Can you think of anything that more imaginatively builds on the words of our Lord that we have read in today's text?

FURTHER STUDY

Psa. 119:18;
John 16:12-15;
1 Cor. 2:7-15

1. How does God open our imagination?

2. Why can we understand spiritual mysteries?

O Father, one of the reasons why I know Your Word is inspired is because it inspires me. Everything comes alive within me as I read it. Help me open up new worlds to others as You open up new worlds to me. In Jesus' name. Amen.

Is this idea biblical?

FOR READING & MEDITATION – PSALM 94:1-23

'Does he who implanted the ear not hear?
Does he who formed the eye not see?' (v.9)

It is possible that you might be saying to yourself at this stage: What biblical foundation is there for believing that God is a story writer? Where does this idea arise in Scripture? Well, I know of no text that explicitly states that God is a story writer, but several verses suggest God is the Author of our story. One is Ephesians 2:10: 'For we are God's workmanship.' This text could also be translated 'We are God's *poem*.' The Greek word used here is *poiema*, from which we get the word 'poem'. Another is 2 Corinthians 3:3: 'You show that you are a letter from Christ.' If we combine these two texts we see that a Christian is to be God's poetry and God's prose. Our lives are to enshrine a divine mystery – poetry – and at the same time express a divine message – prose.

FURTHER STUDY

Psa. 19:1-5;
2 Cor. 3:1-6;
2 Tim. 3:15-17

1. Where does God write His story?

2. What is the purpose of His writings?

There are three occasions recorded in Scripture when God wrote. The first was on Mount Sinai when He inscribed the Ten Commandments on two stone tablets (Deut. 4:13), the second at Belshazzar's feast (Dan. 5:5), and the third when, in the Person of His Son, He wrote in the sand (John 8:6). But it is when I consider the text at the top of this page that I am most convinced God is a story writer.

Whenever I read a story that grips me with its intricate plot and keeps me on the edge of my seat as I follow its twists and turns, I say to myself: If God can gift people with such imagination, what powers of imagination must He Himself possess. He who puts imaginative ideas in the hearts of men and women, is not He the same? If we find excitement in a thrilling novel then what can we expect to find in real life when the Author is none other than the Almighty God?

Gracious Father, help me to truly enter into the excitement of seeing my life not simply as 'a tale to be told' but as a story that is scripted by the world's most innovative and inventive story writer. In Jesus' name. Amen.

FOR READING & MEDITATION – MARK 16:1-8

'He has risen! ... He is going ahead of you into Galilee.' (vv.6-7)

When I first understood that in every believer's life a divine story is being written, it changed my whole approach as a pastor and a counsellor. I have to confess that when I was a young minister I sometimes found it exceedingly dull listening to people talking about their personal problems. Then one day, while preparing an Easter sermon, the Lord spoke to me from the words in today's passage: 'He has risen ... He is going ahead of you into Galilee.'

As I studied this passage the realisation dawned on me that whenever I sat down with someone to listen to their personal problems, *the risen Christ had gone there ahead of me.* He was in that person's life, doing something, saying something, that with the Spirit's help I needed to understand. I realised that my task was much more than to perform the traditional pastoral role, read a few comforting texts and pray; I needed to be alert to the story God was writing in that person's life.

FURTHER STUDY

Esth. 4:1-17

1. What two messages did Mordecai give to Esther?

2. How had God gone ahead in this story?

As soon as I became aware that I was coming in on something that was already happening, and that the events in a person's life should not be looked upon in isolation as problems but as part of a continuing story, counselling changed from being an exacting task into something stimulating and exciting. My task then was to help individuals interpret that story, to encourage them to go back over a line or even a page they had missed or misread, to recover an essential piece of memory. I discovered that the more people understood that beyond the story of their lives a bigger story was unfolding, the more productive counselling became. This is one of the most powerful and transforming of all concepts. We are what we are because of a divine story.

O Lord, I need more light and guidance on this matter. I ask You to wash my eyes and cleanse my heart that I may see. Show me even more clearly that no matter what happens to me, You are always ahead. Amen.

'Prevenient grace'

FOR READING & MEDITATION – PSALM 139:1-6
'You hem me in – behind and before;
you have laid your hand upon me.' (v.5)

Yesterday I said that as soon as I became aware that everyone's life is a story, a complete change took place. Counselling ceased to be an exacting task and became instead something that was stimulating and exciting. As people grasped the idea that their life was a story they changed before my very eyes. Stories enhance, elaborate and develop. One person was so excited that he said to me, 'This idea almost blows my mind. If I am part of a story then nothing that goes on in my life is irrelevant.'

Earlier I mentioned that Eugene Peterson defined counselling as 'listening to someone's story and looking for the movement of God'. Notice the words *the movement of God*. Eugene Peterson, as I pointed out, makes the assumption that at any given moment God is *doing* something. This is a thought I usually introduce when talking to ministers and counsellors. In response, more than one has told me how encouraging it is to realise that as they sit down with someone who is going through a crisis, the Master has gone ahead of them.

FURTHER STUDY

Psa. 139:7-18;
Matt. 28:1-7

1. What did the psalmist understand?

2. What did the angel explain?

I happened to speak about this matter when I was attending a pastors' conference in Singapore. Afterwards a Chinese pastor said to me, 'From now on I will see my hospital visits and counselling sessions in a new light. Whenever I walk into a counselling room or a hospital ward I shall say to myself, "Christ has risen and is going before you."' And then he added, 'I am so intrigued with the idea that the Master is always ahead of me, that when I meet up with His children I am coming in on something that is already in progress. It has revolutionised my ministry.' Theologians call this 'prevenient grace'. Grace is *there* – even before we need it.

O Father, how wonderful it is to realise that Your grace is prevenient – that it is there even before I need it. Help me to trust the transforming power of that grace even when darkness hides it from my sight. In Jesus' name. Amen.

Paul's thorn in the flesh

FOR READING & MEDITATION - 2 CORINTHIANS 12:1-10

'Three times I pleaded with the Lord to take it away from me.' (v.8)

Following on from what I said yesterday, I predict that unless Christian counsellors start to recognise that everyone's life is a story, unless they learn to listen to the story that God is telling in a person's life and go along with it, then they will fail to help people in the way they need to be helped. Overlooking the issue of story is a mistake that is often made. Some time ago I spoke to a young Christian counsellor in training and asked him what goal he set for himself when trying to help others. He replied, 'Well, obviously the removal of the problem.' I suggested to him that Christian counselling must have a much higher goal than that of solving problems; the goal must be *to know God in the problem.*

Imagine that young man sitting down with the apostle Paul who, in today's reading, talks about a problem he was experiencing and describes it as 'a thorn in my flesh'. If his goal was the removal of Paul's problem he would have been working against the purposes of God. Clearly, the Lord was allowing the problem to continue because it served to make Paul a more dependent and defenceless person.

Frequently, I have sat with a person in difficulty and, after seeking to understand what part their problem played in God's story, I have said something like this to them: 'You have to stay with this problem for a little while longer as God is using it to deepen your character and draw you into a closer relationship with Himself.' The highest goal we must have when attempting to help anyone spiritually is not the resolution of the problem but to attempt to understand the story-line that God is writing. Anything less than this will fail to draw out God's plans and purposes.

FURTHER STUDY

2 Cor. 1:3-11; 4:7-18

1. How can we help those in trouble?

2. What did Paul explain?

My Father and my God, thank You for reminding me that the solution of problems is not the highest goal for a Christian. Knowing You is the highest goal. Make me fully aware of this truth, I pray. In Jesus' name. Amen.

'The character on page 29'

FOR READING & MEDITATION - EPHESIANS 1:11-23

' ... according to the plan of him who works out everything in conformity with the purpose of his will ...' (v.11)

It is unrealistic to expect that we will be able to make sense of our lives every step of the way. But that does not mean there is no sense. When I pick up a novel, I become so caught up with the plot that I carry on an imaginary conversation with one of the characters who might appear early in the book (perhaps page 29), and say to him or her, 'You are in a bit of a mess right now, and I wonder how your creator is going to get you out of this.' Then, as I read on and see how, later, the author rescues the character from distress and turns the whole situation around, I go back in my imagination to the character on page 29 and remark, 'There now, you worried unnecessarily didn't you? Things didn't make sense at the time but you were in good hands ... your creator had the way out already planned.'

FURTHER STUDY

Acts 16:16-34

1. How did the apostles respond to trouble?

2. What was the result of their faithful actions?

The character on page 29, could he or she have talked back to me, would not have made sense out of what was happening at that point because he or she was unaware that a bigger story was being written. And life is very much like this. Maybe that is how you are feeling at the moment. Things are happening in your life that just don't make any sense to you. So what have I to say to you? This: *you are only on page 29.* Take heart: up ahead the Divine Author is going to show you the significance of what is happening to you. Remember, He 'works out everything in conformity with the purpose of his will'.

The important thing now is that you trust the Author and play your part well. That may involve helping another person, not letting others down, doing the loving thing even though you don't feel like it. You are part of a story – a much bigger story – and what you do counts – infinitely.

O Father, help me to trust in Your plans at all times. Remind me, I pray, that things are working according to plan - to Your plans, not my plans. In Jesus' name I ask it. Amen.

'Tell me a story'

FOR READING & MEDITATION - MARK 4:21-34

'He did not say anything to them without using a parable.' (v.34)

As a lifelong student of human nature I have come to the conclusion that people have an appetite for stories just as they do for food and drink. Children, as you know, love nothing better at bedtime than to be told a tale. Tonight, in millions of homes all over the world, parents will hear their children ask as they tuck them in for the night, 'Will you tell me a story?'

The desire to be told a story is as old as humanity itself. And when we become adults we do not lose this longing. In this respect we never really grow up. André Malrux, in his book *Anti memoirs*, writes about one of his acquaintances, an elderly and experienced country priest, who said, 'There's no such thing as a grown-up person. We are all children at heart. Some of us know how to disguise it better.' Jesus knew full well the power of a story and used it to great effect in His ministry. The words of our text today make that very clear. In *The Message* Eugene Peterson paraphrases it in this way: 'He was never without a story when he spoke.'

FURTHER STUDY

Matt. 7:24-27;
Luke 10:25-37

1. Why may a story have greater impact than a principle?

2. What did Jesus want His stories to do?

One reason why Jesus used so many stories was because He knew how expert men and women were at arming themselves against the entrance of truth. And human nature doesn't change. Many of us, when we go to church, listen to the sermon that is preached from behind a mental barricade. We are on our guard lest something challenging gets past our defences and touches our conscience. But we listen to stories differently. A story glides unhindered into the very citadel of our mind, and the truth it conveys gains access before we guess its purpose. The story touches our conscience until it stings in confirmation of the point. The flag of surrender goes up and our soul capitulates.

Father, I see that You have given me an appetite for a story. Please give me a greater appreciation of this fact, and may I understand how to use stories in my ministry to others. In Jesus' name I pray. Amen.

Saved - by a story

FOR READING & MEDITATION - 2 SAMUEL 12:1-14

'Then David said to Nathan, "I have sinned against the LORD."' (v.13)

We continue exploring the thought that everyone longs to hear a story. It seems that God has built this desire into the very fabric of our nature. And not just to listen to stories but to tell them also.

The writer Thomas Howard argues – and argues quite successfully – that humankind is a story-telling species, and without story our lives would be much poorer. 'All those stories,' he says, 'about orphan boys who set out on a journey and remember faithfully what they were told by the old beggar woman, who battle with temptation, see through false disguises, and find at the end of their journey that they are not orphans at all but the son of a king – all those stories ring bells in our imagination because that, in fact, is *the* story.' J.R.R. Tolkien, the man who inspired C.S. Lewis and gave him so many ideas for his stories, said, 'Man is a story-telling animal and for this reason God has given him a story to live.'

The passage we have read today shows how God saved David through a story after committing adultery with Bathsheba. It was probably the only way he could have been saved. God sent the prophet Nathan to him with a simple story about a rich man who had large flocks but who stole from a poor man his one little lamb and killed it. David was moved by the story, but because he had deceived himself so completely he could not see in it any application to himself. Almost before the story ended he burst out angrily, 'As surely as the LORD lives, the man who did this deserves to die!' (v.5). The next moment the prophet challenged him with these words: 'You are the man!' (v.7). The lie was exposed. The sophistry was at an end. David had been found out – by a story.

FURTHER STUDY

Gen. 41:15-40

1. How was Egypt saved by a story?

2. What happened to the storyteller?

O Father, I pray that I might never become so self-deceived that I see no application to myself in the truths, principles and stories You have recorded for my benefit in Scripture. Help me develop self-awareness, dear Lord. Amen.

The most appealing stories

FOR READING & MEDITATION - JOSHUA 24:1-18

' ... choose for yourselves this day whom you will serve ...' (v.15)

Our need for a story does not mean we settle for any story. Novelists know that the most appealing ones are those which contain an element of romance and adventure. All good romances and adventure stories contain certain ingredients: the power of a great love, the presence of good and evil, the threat of danger, the eventual judgment of evil, a quest or a journey, and, most importantly, a hero or heroine who passes various tests to save the day or even his or her life.

Many sections of the Bible would lose something if the elements of adventure or romance were absent. Imagine if, in fairy tales, the evil prince or the wicked uncle could sin without impunity, if the dragon could easily be overcome, or if the good prince could save the day by sitting in his castle and studying philosophy. If this were the case then nobody would read them. Those who wrote those ancient stories knew the necessity of including threats of danger, time limits, rescue bids, and so on. People have to make important decisions within a time frame: 'If the stone is not returned to its proper place in the tower before the morning sun strikes the eastern wall, your kingdom and your bride are forfeit.'

FURTHER STUDY

Deut. 30:11-20;
1 Cor. 10:1-13

1. What did Moses and Joshua emphasise?

2. Why does the Bible contain so many stories?

The story before us today is just one of the many Bible passages that show us that out of all the choices we are called upon to make in life, the most important one is to come over onto the Lord's side. But we certainly need to keep in mind that Bible stories, though full of romance and adventure, are not fairy tales but fact. These life-and-death issues are crucial. We must never forget this awesome truth: 'Man is destined to die once, and after that to face judgment' (Heb. 9:27).

Help me, dear Father, to read the Bible not as a page torn from the past but as a mirror that reflects where I am in my own personal journey of faith. May I constantly expose myself to the truths of Your Word. In Christ's name. Amen.

'I will instruct you and teach you in the way you should go ' (v 8)

Some Christians find it difficult to accept that their lives are part of a bigger story. Several years ago, during a counselling session, I tried to convey to a woman who was struggling with the ups and downs of life that through it all a wonderful story was being written. However, she simply could not believe that to be true. 'My life is just a series of random happenings,' she responded, 'with no semblance of sense or design.' Though I tried to explain, she would not listen, and left the counselling room muttering, 'I can't believe it ... I can't believe it.'

After much thought about why some Christians find it difficult to accept the concept of story, I have decided there are several reasons. The first reason, I think, has to do with feelings of self-rejection. It's surprising how many people go through life rejecting themselves. They never felt accepted by those who nurtured them and, believing themselves unworthy of acceptance, they develop a sense of self-hate and self-rejection. They cannot believe that any human being could take an interest in them, let alone God.

FURTHER STUDY

Luke 5:1-11; 15:21-24

1. What did Peter ask of Jesus?

2. How did the Lord respond?

C.S. Lewis, in *Letters to Malcolm: Chiefly on Prayer*, defines prayer in this way: 'Prayer is taking part in the process of being deeply known.' How profound. God knows everything there is to know about an elephant, but the elephant cannot join in the process of being known. Only a person made in the image of God can do that. There are some who cannot joyfully join in the process of being known because they are convinced that if they were deeply known, they would be rejected. They live with a fear of being fundamentally dull. I tell you with conviction that God regards no one in this way. No one.

O Father, what a thrilling thought that through prayer I can join in the process of being known. What a friend You are to me – You know everything there is to know about me yet You love me just the same. Thank You my Father. Amen.

God *is* interested

FOR READING & MEDITATION - PSALM 139:7-24
'How precious to me are your thoughts, O God!' (v.17)

Another reason why some Christians doubt that their lives are part of a bigger story is this: they are not sure that God takes an interest in what happens to them. Many things make it hard for them to believe God takes a personal interest in their affairs – the vastness of space, for example. An astronomer who claims to be a Christian once said something like this to me: 'When I look up at the stars and study the bewildering immensity of space it seems so pitifully naïve to say, "God cares for me, for a tiny person like myself."'

Samuel Chadwick, in his book *The Path to Prayer*, tells of a critic who could not accept the fact that God is at work in the lives of His children, and accosted every believer he met with these words: 'I do not believe you when you say God is interested in the affairs of your life. God is great.' By saying 'God is great' this man meant, of course, that He is too great to be interested in the people who live on planet Earth.

However, we hold to God's personal care and interest in our lives not *in spite* of God's greatness but *because* of it. Though He is far beyond the scope of our thoughts, we dare believe that He stoops to ask for the love of our poor hearts. And even though whirring worlds move at His word, He says to us, 'Be still, and know that I am God' (Psa. 46:10). Managing directors and chief executives may leave some details to their colleagues, but not the Almighty. He does not delegate the responsibility of developing the story-line of our lives. He does this Himself. Let this amazing thought sink into your consciousness today: the God before whom angels veil their faces condescends to involve Himself in the tiniest details of your life.

FURTHER STUDY

Matt. 6:25-34;
10:29-31

1. How did Jesus explain God's interest in us?
2. What was His conclusion?

O God, the thought that You stoop to ask for the love of my heart and have a personal interest in all the details of my life is more than I can take in. Yet I must believe it for it is true. 'I do believe, help me overcome my unbelief!' Amen.

FOR READING & MEDITATION - PHILIPPIANS 3:1-11

'I want to know Christ and the power of his resurrection ...' (v.10)

Consider now a third reason why some people find it difficult to believe that God is sufficiently interested in them to compose a story in their lives: they do not know Him well enough.

Some time ago I was intrigued to read about the rules a person has to follow when presented to the Queen at Buckingham Palace. There are guidelines concerning dress. Lessons in deportment are advised for some. One is expected to be at the palace well ahead of time and to be prepared to wait. It is appreciated if women curtsy and men bow. Contrast this with attendance at the court of heaven – with having an audience with the King of kings. All may come – there is no question of social standing. No introductions are necessary, no seeker is hindered, and no one need delay in order to improve their deportment or dress. Now, as ever, 'The sacrifices of God are a broken spirit; a broken and contrite heart, O God, you will not despise' (Psa. 51:17). Yet how many neglect the privilege and act as though the door is barred against them.

Time and time again I have been somewhat baffled when Christians have told me in a counselling session that they know their families better than they know the Lord. How sad, as Christ can be the Person best known to everyone everywhere! How do we get to know Him? By spending time with Him in prayer and the study of His Word. Those who do not know Him well are the ones who struggle with the idea that He is composing a story in their lives. Of course, discipline is essential. It amazes me that people happily set aside several hours to master some hobby yet blandly suppose they can get to know God during a few sleepy moments at the end of the day.

FURTHER STUDY

Matt. 11:25-30;
Eph. 2:18;
Heb. 4:14-16

1. How can we come to know God?

2. Why is it easier to know God than the Queen?

O Father, how I long to know You better. Yet there is a cost in terms of discipline and time. Help me pay the price, for the knowledge of You is of far greater value than the cost. In Jesus' name. Amen.

The Bible - a story

FOR READING & MEDITATION - EPHESIANS 1:1-10
'... the mystery of his will ... to bring all things in heaven and on earth together under ... Christ.' (vv.9-10)

We move on now to consider the fact that the Bible itself is pre-eminently a story. 'Some people,' says John Stott, 'seem to think of the Bible as trackless jungle, full of contradictions, a tangled undergrowth of unrelated ideas. In fact, it is quite the opposite, for one of the chief glories of the Bible is its coherence.' He adds, 'The whole Bible, from Genesis to Revelation, tells the story of God's sovereign purpose of grace, his master plan of salvation through Christ.' When we read Scripture we are reading a series of stories that blend together to tell an overall story.

Many Christians approach the Bible in the same way they do the internet – as somewhere to go when they are in trouble and need information or advice. They see it only as a book that contains texts they can apply to their daily struggles. There is nothing wrong, of course, in looking up appropriate verses when we are downcast or in need of spiritual help, but we must realise that the Bible has much more to yield than prescriptions on how to stop worrying, how to avoid anger, and so on. First and foremost the Bible is a story – a story of how God is at work, moving from a plan laid down in eternity to a climax within history, and then on beyond time to the future. The story that God is telling in each of our lives is wonderful, but more wonderful still is the story that God tells in the Scriptures.

FURTHER STUDY

Luke 24:13-27; John 20:30-31

1. What did Christ have to explain?

2. Why was John's Gospel written?

Over the years, in my own walk with God, I have found a strange thing: the more I get caught up in the story God is telling in the Bible, the less preoccupied I become with my own personal problems. I can assure you that nothing empowers daily living more than being caught up in *His* story.

O Father, open my eyes to see the big picture which the Bible unfolds. Now I have glimpsed the fact that You have a story that is bigger than my story, I am on fire to know more. Lead me on, dear Father. In Jesus' name. Amen.

The illusion of depth

FOR READING & MEDITATION - JOHN 10:1-21
'I am the gate; whoever enters through me will be saved.' (v.9)

Yesterday we said that the Bible is composed of a series of stories that tell an overall story. Howard Hendricks puts it like this: 'The Bible does not come to us as systematised doctrine but as narrative. *And the story form is as important as the story it tells*' (emphasis mine). In the early days of my ministry I became so preoccupied with analysing the Bible that I missed out on the fact that first and foremost it is a story.

One of the things I have noticed in my study of psychology is that few schools develop the theme of story. Psychology mostly focuses only on what it means to be a 'person' and has no comprehension of what it means to be an heir to a kingdom prepared by God from the beginning of time. And because it misses out on story, it fails to tell the whole story. How refreshing it is to turn from the world of psychology to the world of the Bible and find that Scripture does not deaden our imagination or dull our desire for a story, but actually incites it, encourages it, and supplies us with some of the most exciting stories that have ever been told.

FURTHER STUDY

Col. 2:1-8;
Rev. 3:20

1. Why do we have to be careful?

2. What does Jesus promise?

The disciplines of psychology and sociology have their place in the scheme of things, of course, but in themselves they lack depth. They are like a hall of mirrors, where you see different reflections of yourself. But that is all you see. Eventually you tire of seeing yourself and want to get out, you want to find the door. Jesus talked of Himself as the door or the gate, as we see from today's text. If you are looking for a new world – a world with depth – you will have to find the door. That door is Christ. And going through that door brings you to a much more exciting world than you could ever have imagined.

O Father, how glad I am that I have found that door. Through Your Son I enter a world that surpasses my greatest imagination. Enable me to help others find that door. In Jesus' name I pray. Amen.

FOR READING & MEDITATION - GENESIS 24:1-67
'So they ... asked her, "Will you go with this man?"
"I will go," she said.' (v.58)

We continue reflecting on the thought that most of the Bible is written in story form. If we lose sight of this fact we lose sight of one of God's great abilities for, as G.K. Chesterton put it, 'God is the world's best story-teller.' The stories in Scripture prepare us for great truths. For example, the story we have read today gives us an insight into the wonderful way in which God sent His Holy Spirit into the world to seek out a Bride for His Son. Just as the servant in the story moved under the guidance of God until he at last found the one whom God had elected to be Isaac's wife, so the Spirit has moved (and is moving) through the world, seeking God's elected ones and preparing them for the day when the Bride (the Church) and the Bridegroom (Jesus Christ) will be joined together for all eternity. One of the best descriptions I have heard of the Old Testament is this: *God's wonderful storybook.* It is.

A dangerous trend in today's society is that the value of story-reading is seemingly being lost. It is said that nowadays many children become restless when they are asked to listen to a story being read. It was very different when I was young. In my primary school the last 15 minutes of the day were given over to the reading of a story by our teacher. If someone misbehaved badly, one of the punishments meted out was for the class to be deprived of the daily story. Whenever that happened, the culprit would be so taunted on the way home from school that he or she would think twice before misbehaving again. I will tell you what concerns me about this trend in our society. If Satan destroys our interest in story then I am afraid we will lose our interest in the story of God.

FURTHER STUDY

Matt. 4:4; 11:10; 21:13; 26:31; Acts 8:26-39

1. What did Jesus often do?

2. What prepared the Ethiopian for salvation?

O God, save me from the harmful trends in today's society. You have given me a most wonderful storybook. I neglect it at my cost. Help me never to lose sight of its tremendous and awesome importance. In Christ's name I ask it. Amen.

History - God's story

FOR READING & MEDITATION - GALATIANS 3:15-25

'So the law was put in charge to lead us to Christ that we might be justified by faith.' (v.24)

The Bible tells God's story, and He has given us through the stories in the Bible what Thomas Howard describes as '*the* story of all stories, the only story there is finally'. What is 'the only story there is finally'? Frederick Buechner, in his book *The Complete Literary Guide to the Bible*, summarises the whole message of Scripture in this way: 'God creates, loses and restores.' He goes on to say, 'Christianity is not just a set of presuppositions, or philosophical ideas – it is a story that captures the imagination.'

Dr Larry Crabb sums it up a little differently when he says that God's story consists of seven chapters: (1) God in Trinity; (2) God

FURTHER STUDY

Acts 14:8-17;
17:22-34

1. How did Paul speak to Gentiles?

2. What were the key elements in his message?

and the angels; (3) Evil begins; (4) Paradise created; (5) Paradise lost; (6) Glory revealed through Christ; (7) Glory enjoyed for ever. Paul, in his letter to the Ephesians, captures as no other New Testament writer does the eternal sweep of God's purposes. But here, in today's reading in Galatians, he condenses into just 11 verses the story of the Old Testament – a period of about 2,000 years. It is as if he is describing a mountain range whose peaks are Abraham and Moses, with the highest peak – the Everest – being Jesus Christ. His message is simply this: God's promise to Abraham was confirmed by Moses and fulfilled in Jesus Christ.

In these verses Paul is teaching the unity of the Bible, while at the same time giving us a sense that through history God has been at work, pursuing a purpose that might have been unseen at the time but was nevertheless part of an eternal plan. 'There is a great need in the Church today for a Biblical Christian philosophy of history,' writes a contemporary. There is, for history is *His story*.

O Father, the more I learn about the story You are telling, the more I want to learn. Take me deeper into this subject, dear Lord. And whatever other book I ignore, help me to never ignore Your inspired Word. In Jesus' name. Amen.

Salvation history

FOR READING & MEDITATION - ACTS 3:11-26

'He must remain in heaven until the time comes for God to restore everything, as he promised long ago ...' (v.21)

Yesterday we ended with this statement: 'There is a great need in the Church today for a Biblical Christian philosophy of history.' John Stott says, 'Many of us are so preoccupied with current affairs ... that neither the past nor the future has any great interest for us. We cannot see the wood for the trees. We need to step back and try to take in the whole counsel of God, his everlasting purpose to redeem a people for himself through Jesus Christ.'

Some Christians have little time for the Old Testament as they regard it merely as history. But to understand God's universal epic we must realise that He has been at work not only in the centuries after Christ but in the centuries before also. The ancient Greeks regarded history as a complete circle going nowhere in particular and never reaching an identifiable goal. Similarly, G.N. Clarke, in an inaugural address given at Cambridge University, said, 'There is no secret and no plan in history to be discovered.' André Maurois, a French biographer, wrote, 'The universe is indifferent. Who created it? Why are we here on this puny mud heap spinning in infinite space? I have not the slightest idea, and I am quite convinced no one has.'

FURTHER STUDY

Acts 2:14-41

1. What did Peter explain?

2. What was the result?

The God of the Bible is the God of history – the history of the Old Testament as well as that of the 2,000 years that have passed since Christ was here on the earth. The Almighty, who calls Himself the God of Abraham, Isaac and Jacob (Exod. 3:6), chose Israel out of many nations to be His covenant people, and came to us in the Person of His Son at a recorded moment in history. The history the Bible recounts is 'salvation history', and the salvation it proclaims was achieved by historical events.

Father, I see so clearly that the history Your Word records is 'salvation history'. You have been working through history to achieve Your purposes. Truly, history is Your story. Thank You my Father. In Jesus' name. Amen.

Taking the long look

FOR READING & MEDITATION – HEBREWS 6:13-20

'... God wanted to make the unchanging nature of his purpose
very clear ...' (v.17)

Today we reflect a little more on the fact that our God is the God of history. Henry Ford, in his libel suit with the *Chicago Tribune* in 1919, said, 'History is bunk.' Rudolf Bultmann wrote, 'The question of meaning in history has become meaningless.' And some would echo these words: 'The most accurate chart of the meaning of history is the set of tracks made by a drunken fly with feet wet with ink, staggering across a piece of white paper. They lead nowhere and reflect no pattern of meaning.' Are they right? Of course not. These views fail to see things from God's perspective, from an *eternal* point of view. When we look at the fragments of history they tell us very little, but when we take 'the long look' we can see, as C.S. Lewis put it, that 'History is a story written by the finger of God.'

FURTHER STUDY

Acts 7:40-60

1. How did Stephen embrace his past, present and future with story?

2. Why did people not like his story?

Historians and cosmologists who see the past as merely one senseless crisis after another have no answer to the question: Where have we come from and where are we going? And because they consider history has no sense or pattern, they soon become prey to the philosophy of existentialism, which embraces the present to the exclusion of both the future and the past. Yet amid the tides of modern philosophies the believing Christian stands fast and realises that despite all the difficulties sin has caused, there is a divine design which runs throughout history.

Rest assured, my friend. Pause and consider the bigger picture: history is not a random succession of events, each effect having its cause, and each cause having its effect, yet the whole betraying no overall pattern. The God revealed in the Bible is working to a plan and is accomplishing all things according to the purpose of His will (see Eph. 1:11).

Father, forgive me if I am so taken up with the present that neither the past nor the future has any great interest for me. Help me step back and take in the whole purpose of God – to take the long look. In Jesus' name. Amen.

Invitation to a wedding

FOR READING & MEDITATION - REVELATION 19:1-10

'... the wedding of the Lamb has come, and his bride has made herself ready.' (v.7)

Having spent three days reflecting on the fact that history is *His story* – God's story – we move on now to ask ourselves: What exactly is the overall story which the Bible is telling? What is the big story of God? It is a *love story*. This is the thought we touched on a few days ago when we looked at the account of Abraham sending his servant Eliezer to find a bride for Isaac (Gen. 24:1–67), but now I would like to deal with it in more detail.

George Macdonald wrote, 'When we unravel the facts of history, together with the many statements of Scripture, we stumble across a love story of immense magnitude – the love of the Father for the Son, and the love of the Son for His Bride.' A.W. Tozer put it like this: 'The end which God had in mind for His universe when first He created it was to provide His Son with a Bride. This and this alone unfolds the meaning behind all history and makes it comprehensible.' So the big story of God – His universal epic – is essentially a romantic one.

God's concern to provide a Bride for His Son is laid down in the types and shadows of the Old Testament. It is unfolded more fully for us by the apostle Paul, and brought into final focus in the passage we have read today. The greatest event in the eternity to come will be the wedding supper of the Lamb. Many years ago the poet T.S. Eliot penned these depressing words: 'This is the way the world ends. Not with a bang but with a whimper.' For Christians, the end of all things will not be a whimper, but a wedding. We will 'rejoice and be glad ... for the wedding of the Lamb has come'. We who have been wooed by Christ and won to Him will one day be wed to Him. Hallelujah!

FURTHER STUDY

Matt. 22:1-14; 25:1-13

1. What is required of wedding participants?

2. What may prevent us responding to God's wedding invitation?

O Father, this is something I can hardly take in. It would be enough to be saved from hell and given a place in heaven. But to be joined to You, to be one with You, almost blows my mind. All I can say is: Thank You dear Lord. Thank You. Amen.

The big story of God

FOR READING & MEDITATION - EPHESIANS 5:22-33

'This is a profound mystery - but I am talking about Christ and the church.' (v.32)

We continue meditating on the fact that the universal epic God is writing is a love story - of His concern to provide a Bride for His Son. All of us are familiar with the fairy story that tells of a princess who kisses a frog and by so doing turns him into a handsome prince. God's big story is about a Bridegroom touching the lives of stubborn, independent sinners such as you and me, and by His grace turning us into people fit to be joined in marriage to Him, to be His companions for all eternity.

The apostle Paul, when talking about the fact that a husband and wife become one flesh, goes on to say, 'This is a profound mystery - but I am talking about Christ and the church.' What is the 'mystery' that engages his attention here? It is the 'mystery' that just as a married couple become one flesh, so the Church will be one with Christ in eternity. Not a buddy but a bride, not a pal but a partner.

FURTHER STUDY

Isa. 62:1-5;
Hosea 2:14-3:1

1. What causes God to rejoice?

2. How would the Israelites refer to the Lord?

Non-Christian historians cannot conceive that behind the universe is a love story. Once, on a plane, I found myself sitting next to an historian. During the course of our conversation I asked the man what lessons he drew from his study of history. He paused for a moment and said, 'There seems no sense in history.' As I tried to explain to him that through all the seeming chaos a divine scheme is being worked out - a romantic one - he looked at me in amazement. Obviously keen to avoid further discussion, he shuffled his papers and said that though he would like to talk more about the matter, he had a lot of work to catch up on. When, at the end of the flight he told me he was catching another plane and going on somewhere else, I could not help but think: I wonder where.

O Father, what a prospect - what a story! We who were deep-dyed sinners but are now washed and made clean through the blood of Your Son, are to be joined with You for ever. I still can't get over it, dear Lord. Blessed be Your name for ever. Amen.

A divine intimation?

FOR READING & MEDITATION – GENESIS 2:15-25

'Then the Lord God made a woman from the rib he had taken out of the man, and he brought her to the man.' (v.22)

For one more day we reflect on the thought that God's chief purpose from the beginning of time was to provide His Son with a Bride. There appears to be an intimation of this truth in the story of Eve's creation from Adam, recounted in our reading today. A great Welsh preacher of the nineteenth century, Dr Cynddylan Jones, expressed this viewpoint: 'What happened in the first few pages of the Bible is a dress rehearsal for what takes place in the last few pages of the Bible, when the Church, the Bride of Christ, who was *in* Him and came *out* of Him, will be joined *to* Him in a marriage that will last for all eternity.'

In these words he was saying that the creation of the woman is a picture of the Christian Church. First, the woman was in the man – conceptually at least. Then she was taken out of him when God opened up Adam's side. Around the rib that was taken from him God 'built' a woman. Lastly, God gave the woman back to the man, and saw that as the act of holy matrimony (v.24).

Isn't this creative act similar to the conception, creation and consummation of Christ's Bride, the Church? In Ephesians 1:4 we are told that God saw us *in* Christ before the foundation of the world. In verse 7 we see that we have redemption through His blood – the blood, you remember, that came from His riven side when a soldier pierced Him with a spear (John 19:34). In Ephesians chapter 5 we read that we who were *in* Him and came *out* of Him will be joined yet again *to* Him.

Cynddylan Jones said, 'God couldn't wait to tell the world how He planned to provide a Bride for His Son, and so He built the truth in typological form into the original creation.' Was he right? You decide.

FURTHER STUDY

Ruth 4:1-17;
Songs 4:7-15

1. How are Boaz and Ruth like Christ and the Church?

2. How would Christ speak to His Bride?

My Father and my God, whether or not Your purpose when You created Eve from Adam was to typify what I have read about today, one thing is sure: my salvation came from You and my destiny is to be joined to You. Hallelujah! Amen.

The central character

FOR READING & MEDITATION - MATTHEW 1:18-25
'This is how the birth of Jesus Christ came about ...' (v.18)

There is usually a central character in a story – the star or headliner of the story. And the central character in God's big story is Jesus. Some think of Jesus as the central character of the New Testament only, but He is the central character of the Old Testament too. 'To see the story of Jesus as confined only to the New Testament,' says one commentator, 'is to misunderstand the purpose of the Bible.'

No doubt you were relieved today's reading started at verse 18 and not verse 1. Yet Matthew gives our Lord's genealogy for a particular reason. He will not allow us to read about Jesus' birth before we have ploughed through a list of historical figures because until we see Christ in the context of His ancestors we will not properly understand His story. Jewish genealogies established the right to belong to the community of God's people. Ancestry gave people their identity and status. And Jesus' very mission necessitated Him belonging to the people who were to bring blessing to the earth; He was the fulfilment of all the Old Testament promises that related to the Messiah. Jesus has to be seen in the light of a bigger story that goes back many centuries.

FURTHER STUDY

Gen. 3:14-15;
Isa. 53:1-12;
Mal. 3:1-4

1. How do we see Christ in Genesis and Isaiah?
2. How do we see Christ in Malachi?

The Old Testament, says Chris Wright in his book *Knowing Jesus through the Old Testament*, tells the story which Jesus completes. 'Without the Old Testament,' he claims, 'then Jesus quickly loses reality and either becomes a stained-glass window figure – colourful but static and undemanding – or a tailor's dummy that can be dressed to suit the current fashion.' Jesus without the bigger story would not be the Person we know He is. Our Lord is no identikit figure; He is a real man – though of course much more than a man.

Lord Jesus Christ, while I rejoice that You are the central character of Scripture, I am more thankful still that You are the central character in my life. Without You life would not be worth living. Amen.

FOR READING & MEDITATION - LUKE 19:1-10

'For the Son of Man came to seek and to save what was lost.' (v.10)

We continue reflecting on the thought which we started to consider yesterday, namely that Jesus is the central character – the star – of God's story. The glory goes not to the ones who are saved but to the one who saves. Some time ago, I watched a television programme featuring the remarkable story of a woman who was saved from drowning on an Australian beach. The man who saved her was not a life-saver – just an ordinary Australian citizen who had been walking along the beach with his dog. He couldn't even swim. However, when he saw the woman was in difficulty he raced to get a lifebelt, waded into the sea as far as he could, and threw it to her. Fortunately she managed to grasp it, and because a rope was attached to the lifebelt he was able to pull her safely to the shore.

A television crew happened to be close by and immediately started filming and interviewing the rescuer. While one cameraman focused on the crowds who had gathered around the man to congratulate him, another zoomed in on the woman who had just been saved – sitting all alone, gathering her breath. No comment was given and no comment was needed. The glory, as I said above, goes not to the ones who are saved but to the one who saves.

People who don't know Christ often wonder why we make so much of Jesus. If only they could know the joy of abundant living, of sins forgiven, and, as the old hymn so beautifully puts it, 'of hell subdued and heaven begun'. A preacher I once heard, declared, 'Jesus is my hero'. At first I was slightly offended by the expression. But the more I thought about it the more I realised he was right. Jesus is not only God's hero; He is my hero and role model too.

FURTHER STUDY

1 Sam. 8:19-20; 18:6-7

1. What do many people look for?

2. How does Jesus fulfil the role of a true hero?

Lord Jesus Christ, how can I ever thank You enough for saving me and for being such a wonderful Saviour? I give You all the praise for my salvation – and will do for ever. Amen.

The only Saviour

FOR READING & MEDITATION - ACTS 4:1-12

'Salvation is found in no-one else, for there is no other name under heaven ... by which we must be saved.' (v.12)

Today we meditate further on the fact that Jesus is the hero of God's big story. Other religions hold Jesus in high honour, but they do not regard Him as the centre of God's purposes. Hindus gladly recognise Him as an 'avatar' (incarnation) of Vishnu. Muslims acknowledge Him as one of the great prophets whose virgin birth, sinless life, acts of kindness, miracles, and return one day to this earth are all affirmed in the Qur'an. Jews, who reject Jesus as the Messiah, still write of Him as a man of outstanding character. Karl Marx, who was fiercely critical of religion and regarded it as opium that drugged the oppressed into tolerating the injustices of those in power, nevertheless had a high regard for Jesus.

FURTHER STUDY

Acts 17:22-34;
1 Tim. 2:5-6

1. Why were the religious Athenians confused?

2. What makes Jesus unique?

Some years ago I spoke to a group of non-Christian students on the theme 'The Historic Jesus'. After I had finished, the young chairman got up and called for 'Three cheers for Jesus'. I felt sad that somehow my point had been missed, for it is not 'three cheers' Jesus wants but the homage of our hearts.

Jesus Christ is not one Saviour among others; He is the *only* Saviour. He is not one of Hinduism's 330 million gods or one of the 40 prophets recognised in the Qur'an. He is not even, in the words of John Stott, 'Jesus the Great, as you might say Napoleon the Great or Alexander the Great.' He continues, 'To us He is the only; He is simply Jesus. Nothing could be added to that; He is unique.' In an age when schools teach that all religions have equal value, we should never forget that Christianity is not one faith among many other faiths; it is in a category all by itself. Christianity is not a religion but a relationship. Jesus Christ is not *a* Saviour, He is the *only* Saviour.

Father, save me from being carried along by the pluralism which is so rife in today's society and from losing sight of the fact that Jesus is the *only* Saviour. Help me be true to Scripture, but without arrogance. In Jesus' name I pray. Amen.

The star of the story

'And a voice from heaven said, "This is my Son, whom I love ..."' (v.17)

For one more day we consider the implications of the fact that Jesus is the central character in God's great story. There are some who like to downplay Jesus' role, and who regard Christianity as just an ethical system. They speak about the fine principles of the Sermon on the Mount, the Golden Rule, and so on, forgetting that without Christ's presence in one's life the principles given in the Sermon on the Mount are impossible to keep. As I have said before, when Jesus presented the principles outlined in the Sermon on the Mount He was not saying, 'Live like this and you will become a Christian'; what He was saying was, 'Become a Christian and you will live like this'. You cannot extract Jesus' teaching on morality and present it in isolation.

It makes no sense to talk about the Christian ethic and ignore Christ. You cannot take the words of Jesus and pretend that they came from the lips of any other person. How would it sound if any other man, however great he may be, were to talk about himself in the way Jesus did? Think, for instance, how it would sound if the British prime minister were to say, 'I am the resurrection and the life.' Or if some other good-living world-renowned personality were to claim, 'Before Abraham was born, I am.' That is not their story. Those lines belong to one Person and one Person alone – our Lord Jesus Christ.

Those who regard Christianity as nothing more than moral teaching miss the point. 'Christianity,' said one theologian, 'is Christ.' On Him all the Old Testament truths converge and from Him all the New Testament truths emerge. He is the centre of gravity of the Bible, the hub of the evangel, *the star of God's story*.

FURTHER STUDY

John 5:16-18; Rev. 5:1-14

1. Why did the Jews try to kill Jesus?

2. Who is worshipped in heaven?

Father, with great humility I confess it: Jesus is not only the star of Your story but the star of my story also. Without Him I am nothing. Just as You rejoiced in Your Son so do I rejoice in Him too. Amen.

Finitude linked to infinity

FOR READING & MEDITATION – JOHN 5:16-30

'Jesus said ... "My Father is always at his work ... and I, too,
am working."' (v.17)

Having recognised the centrality of Jesus Christ in God's big story, we now consider the question: What happens if we fail to grasp the sense of story, which is the pre-eminent theme of Scripture? One thing that will occur is this: we will get caught up in our own story and become preoccupied with self rather than the Saviour. The philosopher Jean-Paul Sartre said that no finite point can adequately serve as its own context. If I take the finite point of my own story, I cannot get meaning without a larger context. God's bigger story puts my own story in context. My finitude is linked to infinity. I must ask myself: Do I see a story that is much bigger than my own personal story or do I simply see myself as the beginning and end of the story?

FURTHER STUDY

2 Kings 5:1-15;
Eph. 2:10

1. How was a humble slave girl linked to infinity?

2. What has God planned?

Another thing that can happen if we fail to grasp the sense of story is that we lose the awareness of being drawn into the action of God. The Almighty is at work in the world. The verse that is our text today makes that quite clear. Notice that the words 'is always at his work' and 'am working' are in the present tense. What work is the Father engaged in? A whole range of things, of course, but part of His work is developing His salvation story – a story in which you and I have a special part.

Every believer is included in God's story, is travelling towards Him, and being drawn closer to Him. Are you not aware of a sense of journeying as you move from day to day – a sense that you are being shaped, moulded, discipled and fitted into His plan? If you do not have this sense of being caught up in the action of God then stop everything right now, get down on your knees, and reflect on what I have been saying over these past few days.

Father, if I am slow to learn the lesson that my life is part of a bigger story, an eternal story, please forgive me. Help me look at this truth not through the eyes of chilling doubt but through the eyes of kindling faith. Amen.

Driven – or drawn?

FOR READING & MEDITATION – MARK 12:18–27

'Jesus replied, "Are you not in error because you do not know the
Scriptures or the power of God?"' (v.24)

Yesterday we mentioned two things that are likely to happen if
we fail to grasp a sense of story: we will become preoccupied
with our own self, and we will deprive ourselves of the knowledge
and thrill of being caught up in the action of God. Yet another thing
that will happen is this: we will treat the Bible as an exegetically
precise system and miss its real power. Eugene Peterson puts this
thought in a compelling way when he says, 'When we fail to
develop a sense of story then we start applying the Bible, taking
charge of a verse or doctrine or moral with which we intend to fix
some fragment of ourselves.'

But isn't that what we are supposed to do with the
Bible – apply it? Certainly we should apply biblical
teaching and principles, but we miss the essential
meaning of the Bible if that is all we do. The ancient
Sadducees were studious readers of the Scriptures, but
they overlooked their main purpose; they were good at
alighting on specific texts but, as our reading today tells
us, they failed to understand what was really being said.
Many Christians' lives are flawless in terms of morality
but yet are flat in terms of passion. They know how
to apply particular Bible texts to life's issues but they
cannot see beyond the texts of Scripture to the bigger story. They
are driven people rather than drawn people.

FURTHER STUDY

Mark 16:14-20;
2 Cor. 5:11-15

1. How did the
disciples apply
the words of
Jesus?

2. What drove
Paul?

Christianity first and foremost, as we have already said, is not an
ethical system; it is a story. The story is mainly about the Master
– who He is, where He came from, what He has done, and what He
is still doing. 'The things we Christians do,' says William Kilpatrick,
'we do not so much for ethical reasons but because we are caught
up in a story.'

**Father, help me examine myself today to see whether I am driven
by an inner urge to conform to a code or drawn to live for You
because I am caught up in the story You are telling. In Jesus'
name I ask this. Amen.**

No sense of story

FOR READING & MEDITATION - JOSHUA 4:1-24

'No sooner had they set their feet on the dry ground than the waters of the Jordan returned to their place ...' (v.18)

I have no hesitation in saying that the Christian life without a sense of story tends to lack vibrancy. What I am about to describe now will be regarded by some as over-imaginative, but others will, I am sure, recognise that it is true.

Christians go to church on Sunday, and for a while the waters of chaos and confusion roll back as they focus on the worship of God. For an hour or two truth clears away the fog that swirls in their minds and, like the Israelites, they prepare to go out to possess the land.

The pastor shakes hands with people as they leave and, as he does so, touches hands that are trembling with anxiety, resentment, guilt and many other emotions. A mother, perhaps, has just discovered her son is on drugs. An executive is about to be made redundant. A wife has discovered her husband is having an affair. A family is facing the death of a loved one. How many believers find within hours of getting home that the waters are again overflowing the banks, as in the passage we have read today? If Christians have no sense of story – of what one commentator describes as 'knowing that our private histories are grafted into the stock of salvation history' – the waters soon rush back in waves of confusion and distress.

FURTHER STUDY

Isa. 43:1-11;
John 9:1-7

1. What is God's promise?

2. What did Jesus explain?

How I wish this message was preached from more pulpits: God is at work, taking everything that goes on in our lives and weaving it into His salvation story. If we do not view the details of our existence as chapters in God's story then we will easily fall prey to gloom and pessimism. I know of nothing that enables us to possess the land of our spiritual inheritance more effectively than the knowledge that our personal stories are being woven into God's own story.

Gracious Father, open my eyes that I might see - really see - that my personal story is congruent with the story of Your salvation. Help me, my Father, for I must get hold of this. In Jesus' name. Amen.

Everyone has a part

FOR READING & MEDITATION - RUTH 1:1-14

'... there was a famine ... a man from Bethlehem ... together with his wife and two sons, went to live ... in ... Moab.' (v.1)

Yesterday we commented that one of the saddest things that can happen to a Christian is failing to recognise that our personal story is congruent with the story God is telling. Far too many Christians, when presented with the fact that they are part of God's salvation story, respond by saying something like this: 'I can't believe that my life has any place in the eternal scheme of things. I am too small and insignificant to have any part in God's cosmic purpose.' Their guilt, fears and inferiority combine to make them feel that a place in God's universal purposes may be right for others but not for them. How do we break free from such a jaundiced outlook?

A helpful suggestion, which we are about to follow, is to dip into the Old Testament story of Ruth. This book, perhaps more than any other, helps us understand that our lives are chapters in the epic of God's salvation history. The interesting thing about the book of Ruth is that there are no outstanding personalities in the narrative – no kings, prophets, judges or priests. It is a simple, ordinary story about three widows and a farmer whose personal experiences of everyday life are woven into God's universal epic.

The great characters of the Bible, such as Abraham, Isaac, Jacob, Joseph, Solomon, David and Daniel, can be intimidating to ordinary people. 'Surely,' they say, 'there is no way that I can be included in such a star-studded cast.' The story of Ruth, as we shall see, gives the lie to such a viewpoint. Every detail of every believer's life is part of a universal epic – the story of salvation. And you are as much an integral part of that as are Abraham, Isaac, Jacob, Joseph, Solomon, David, Daniel – and Ruth.

FURTHER STUDY

1 Cor. 12:1-14

1. What did Paul want us to know?

2. What is common to us all and what is different?

O Father, can it really be true that the details of my life are being tied in to the story of salvation ... that I am a part of Your big story? It sounds too good to be true, but then too good not to be true. Show me more, dear Lord. Amen.

Three funerals and a wedding

FOR READING & MEDITATION - RUTH 1:15-22

'Don't call me Naomi ... Call me Mara, because the Almighty has made my life very bitter.' (v.20)

Now we look in closer detail at the lives of some very ordinary people to see how their personal stories were woven into God's universal epic. Over the years I have heard and read many interesting comments on Ruth, but none so wonderful as this: 'Ruth was an inconsequential outsider whose life is essential for telling the complete story of salvation.' A woman who was not born into the Jewish faith – an outsider – became integrated into the larger story of God's people.

Those who think God only weaves into the tapestry of His eternal purposes the big names of the Bible need to study the book of Ruth, for her simple but delightful story is proof to the contrary. It is a story about a famine, three funerals and a wedding! But let's begin at the beginning.

FURTHER STUDY

1 Cor. 12:14-31

1. Why is no one insignificant?

2. How is the Church similar to, yet different from, a sports team?

The story starts with the announcement of a famine in the land of Judah. In the small town of Bethlehem a man by the name of Elimelech takes his wife Naomi and their two sons, and goes to live for a while in the land of Moab. After a period of time Elimelech dies, and his two sons marry Moabite women. Later the two sons also die, leaving Naomi and her daughters-in-law in difficult circumstances. Naomi decides to return to Bethlehem, and Ruth, one of her daughters-in-law, pleads to be allowed to accompany her.

When, after a ten-year absence, Naomi finally arrives back in Bethlehem, her return creates a great stir in the town. Naomi, however, can only respond to their excitement with words of lament: 'I went away full, but the LORD has brought me back empty' (v.21). That might sound a very negative thing to say, but her very emptiness is woven into the plot and becomes, as we shall discover, the occasion for God's providence.

Father, I see that negative feelings or even complaints that are voiced do not preclude us from contributing to Your story. You treat our complaints seriously. For that I am deeply grateful. Amen.

FOR READING & MEDITATION - JEREMIAH 20:7-18
'O LORD, you deceived me, and I was deceived; you overpowered me
and prevailed.' (v.7)

Yesterday we ended with the thought that Naomi's emptiness was woven into God's plot and became the occasion for God's providence. Naomi's complaint, we noted, was taken seriously; it was not deleted from the story, toned down or spiritualised. The point must not escape us that Naomi's complaint becomes, in fact, part of the story. Complaints are quite common in Scripture. Jeremiah's – the one in our reading today – is probably the best known.

Edward F. Campbell, in the comments on Ruth which he makes in the *Anchor Bible*, says, 'Not only is complaint tolerated by God but it can even be the proper stance of a person who takes God seriously: petulant Jonah, earnest Jeremiah, persistent Job – Naomi stands in the company.' If there had been an editorial deletion of Naomi's complaint – if it had been judged unsuitable for a story about salvation – then the account would not have been an entirely factual one. Though she viewed herself as empty, she was given a symbolic filling when Ruth returned from Boaz with a generous gift of barley for her. 'You can't go back empty-handed to your mother-in-law!' Boaz had told Ruth (3:17, *The Message*).

FURTHER STUDY

Ruth 2:1-23

1. How did God guide Ruth?

2. Why did Boaz admire and bless Ruth?

Later we see that Naomi's emptiness is reversed when, after the birth of Obed, Ruth's first child, the women of Bethlehem cry, 'Naomi has a son!' (4:17). Not Ruth, notice, but Naomi. Notice too that when Naomi first uttered her complaint God did not immediately intervene and give her an explanation of His ways. Instead she found herself, as one commentator describes it, 'in a living, developing set of relationships that extend into the future'. Her negative feelings were not edited out of God's story but integrated into it.

O Father, I am glad that You did not edit Naomi's complaint out of the narrative or judge it unsuitable to be included in a story about salvation. You took it and used it to demonstrate Your providence. How wonderful. Amen.

Speaking your own lines

FOR READING & MEDITATION – RUTH 3:1-18

'Spread the corner of your garment over me, since you are a
kinsman-redeemer.' (v.9)

We have seen that Naomi became included in the story of salvation outlined for us in the book of Ruth by way of a complaint. Today we ask: How did Ruth enter the story? *By making clear what she wanted.* By this stage Naomi had informed Ruth that Boaz was a close relative and a kinsman-redeemer. They knew, therefore, that if they handled the situation correctly then they would be rescued from poverty and that Ruth would have a husband. Thus Naomi coaches Ruth: 'Wash and perfume yourself, and put on your best clothes. Then go down to the threshing-floor ... When he lies down, note the place where he is lying. Then go and uncover his feet ... He will tell you what to do' (vv.3–4).

FURTHER STUDY

Mark 10:46-52;
John 20:24-29

1. Why was Bartimaeus healed?

2. What was the result of Thomas speaking his mind?

Ruth does exactly what her mother-in-law suggests with one exception. She does not wait for Boaz to tell her what to do; instead, she takes the initiative and tells *him* what to do: 'Spread the corner of your garment over me, since you are a kinsman-redeemer.' This was a symbolic way of saying, 'Will you marry me?' Ruth's intervention may seem somewhat forward, but as one commentator puts it, 'Being in God's story does not mean passively letting things happen to us. It does not mean dumb submission, nor blind obedience.'

There are times when it is right to speak our own lines, not just parrot those that have been given us by others. Be assured of this: you will not be excluded from God's story when you speak the lines that come from your own heart rather than those are imposed on you by others. Of course, it is right to allow ourselves to be coached by parents, schoolteachers and others, but there are times when we must be ready to ask for what we want – to speak our own lines.

Father, I see that just as You accept complaint, so You acknowledge creativity also. You do not reject those who make up their own lines. And for that, too, I am again deeply thankful. Amen.

Not a passive player

FOR READING & MEDITATION - EZEKIEL 16:1-14
'I spread the corner of my garment over you and covered
your nakedness.' (v.8)

You may have thought that a comment I made yesterday –
that Ruth's action of asking Boaz to spread the corner of his
garment over her was a symbolic way of asking him to marry her
– is somewhat far-fetched. But this language is used again in our
text for today in connection with God's marriage contract with
Israel: 'Later I passed by, and when I looked at you and saw that
you were old enough for love, I spread the corner of my garment
over you and covered your nakedness.' By her action Ruth was
signalling that she was putting herself under the protection of
Boaz. The Amplified Bible translates Ruth's request in this way:
'Spread your wing [of protection] over your maidservant,
for you are a next of kin.'

Evidence of this custom is given by commentators
such as Edward F. Campbell, who refer to the ancient
Arabic custom of placing of a garment over a woman
as a symbolic claim to marriage. When I visited Bahrain
some years ago, I was told that some Arabs still practise
this symbolic gesture when selecting a wife.

I make the point once again: for Ruth to be in God's
story it did not follow that she had to be a passive player.
Even though she is a foreigner (six times in the story she is called
a Moabitess), and had been born outside the boundaries of the
covenant nation of Israel, she enters the central action of the story
when she steps out of the role in which she had been placed by
others and, in addition to doing what Naomi had instructed, takes
the initiative and speaks her own lines. And the consequences of
Ruth's courageous actions are astounding. She takes her place in
history as the great-grandmother of King David and an ancestor
of Jesus Christ, the Messiah.

**FURTHER
STUDY**

1 Sam. 14:1-23

1. How did
Jonathan take
the initiative?

2. What was the
result?

O Father, although I am grateful for those who have coached me
in spiritual things, help me not to just repeat the statements of
others but, whenever necessary, to step out and speak the words
I feel compelled to speak. In Jesus' name. Amen.

'Mr So and So'

FOR READING & MEDITATION - RUTH 4:1-4

'... no-one has the right to do it except you, and I am next in line.' (v.4)

Another important player in the narrative we are considering is, of course, Boaz. How did Boaz become part of God's salvation story? By accepting responsibility. Boaz was a wealthy relative of Naomi's husband, and is seen in the story as a perfect gentleman and a man of outstanding character: solid, honest and upright. His name means 'strength' or 'substance', and he is the hero of the story. He agreed to marry Ruth according to the custom of levirate marriage by which the nearest male relative married a man's widow (see Deut. 25:5–10).

There was, however, a kinsman who was more closely related to Ruth – an unnamed character with whom Boaz bargained. Boaz succeeded in persuading this man to give up his right to marry Ruth. Had he wished, Boaz could have avoided marrying Ruth and still kept his good name since there was another man who had a greater responsibility than he had. One commentator says of him, 'Boaz could have kept the letter of the law by referring the matter of Ruth to the nearer kinsman, "Mr So and So". The scene at the city gate in which the redeemer obligations are worked out makes it clear that Boaz, "the man of substance", will live up to his name.'

FURTHER STUDY

Mark 7:1-13;
2 Cor. 3:1-6

1. Why may keeping the letter of the law be wrong?

2. How can we live by the spirit of the law?

In the story we see that Boaz had an opportunity to act responsibly and he seized it, not simply because it was expected of him but because he wanted to. He was the kind of man who was not content to live by the letter of the law, but one who sought ways to put his wealth and position to work on behalf of others. This is demonstrated not only by his treatment of Ruth but also by his concern for the welfare of his workers. In Boaz we find a man who lived not by the letter of the law but by the spirit of it.

O Father, save me from seeking to conform to the letter of the law and not going beyond it. Help me to look for creative ways in which I can put all my gifts and abilities to work on behalf of others. In Jesus' name I ask it. Amen.

That is how it should be ...

FOR READING & MEDITATION - RUTH 4:5-8
'So the kinsman-redeemer said to Boaz, "Buy it yourself."
And he removed his sandal.' (v.8)

We must not overlook the fact that the story of Ruth is set in 'the days when the judges ruled' (1:1), a period of Israel's history when 'Israel had no king; everyone did as he saw fit' (Judg. 21:25). It was a time when 'might was right' – 'an era', says one commentator, 'in which strength became bullying and domineering and people took care of themselves at the expense of the widows and the poor'. How refreshing, therefore, to discover in such turbulent times a man like Boaz who went beyond the letter of the law and sought to use his wealth and position for the good of others who were not so well off.

In Israel, every woman was the responsibility of the man who was her next of kin. According to family law, the nearest relative had certain obligations. These included providing an heir, when a man had died childless, to carry on his name, and buying land to keep it in the family. Boaz was one of those in line to take responsibility for Ruth, as Naomi's comment reveals: 'That man is our close relative; he is one of our kinsman-redeemers' (2:20).

Edward F. Campbell describes the role of a redeemer in this way: 'to function on behalf of persons and their property within the circle of the larger family ... to take responsibility for the unfortunate and stand as their supporters and advocates ... to care for those who may not have justice done for them'. Because Boaz took on the responsibility that came his way, lived up to his name, and did more than was required of him by the law, he became a leading character in a story that has made his name immortal. The energy that pulsed through his soul was other-centred. That is how it should be with everyone who is part of God's story.

FURTHER STUDY

Gen. 44:1-33;
Heb. 7:24-25;
1 John 2:1-2

1. How did Judah assume responsibility for his brother?

2. How does Jesus assume responsibility for us?

My Father and my God, help me to live out my part in Your story by taking up every responsibility that is presented to me with enthusiasm and a generous spirit. Make me a truly other-centred person. In Jesus' name Amen.

FOR READING & MEDITATION - RUTH 4:9-12

'I have also acquired Ruth ... as my wife, in order to maintain the name of the dead with his property ...' (v.10)

For one more day we reflect on the role Boaz has in the story of God's salvation as it is narrated in the book of Ruth. Here is a man in whose heart burns a desire not merely to keep to the letter of the law, but to give *all* of himself in the service of others. His concern was not to discover what was the *least* he could do, but what was the *most* he could do. His life motto could have been (to borrow Oswald Chambers' beautiful words) *my utmost for His highest.*

The theme of redemption is highlighted in this story by the fact that Boaz was not only conversant with the details of an old

FURTHER STUDY

Matt. 5:41-42;
Acts 20:22-24;
2 Cor. 11:21-33

1. What does the Lord ask of us?

2. What did Paul offer the Lord?

Mosaic law, but had a generous enough heart to go beyond it. The name Boaz, we said, means 'substance' or 'strength'. There are some people who use their strength and substance simply to maintain themselves, possibly at the expense of others. The question each one of us must answer is this: Where is the energy that drives our personalities being directed – towards ourselves or others?

Some Christians regard their wealth as theirs by right and never consider the fact that with rights come responsibilities. I like what one commentator says concerning Boaz: 'When he decided to act in this way [in generosity rather than the mere keeping of the law] God's "wings" (2:12-13) are experienced in the story through the "wings" of Boaz (3:9).' Again I say: more is expected of us than keeping to the letter of the law. We are expected to go the second mile (see Matt. 5:41). And if you will forgive a change of metaphor here: when the Holy Spirit indwells us it is expected that out of our innermost beings will flow not trickles or rivulets but streams of living water (see John 7:38). *Streams!*

Loving heavenly Father, may what You pour into me also flow out from me. You are not niggardly in what You give to me; help me not to be niggardly in what I give out to others. In Jesus' name I ask it. Amen.

Anyone can get in

FOR READING & MEDITATION - RUTH 4:13-17

'And they named him Obed. He was the father of Jesse,
the father of David.' (v.17)

There is a very wonderful purpose behind God's direction to include the story of Ruth in the canon of Scripture. This short book shows us so clearly the way in which God takes ordinary people and lifts them out of their ordinariness into the drama of His universal epic. There are, of course, characters other than Naomi, Ruth and Boaz in the book, and though most of them are unnamed, they are also important: the young man who was foreman of the harvesters, for example, the nearer kinsman in chapter 4, the anonymous women who sang 'Naomi has a son' in 4:17, and so on. They also get into the story. Who knows whether, if the spotlight could be turned on them, they too could tell stories which, though perhaps not as dramatic as Ruth's, nevertheless have significance.

But we must come now to the concluding words of the book, particularly the verse that is our text for today. This verse appears to make a straightforward genealogical statement, but what a wealth of truth lies within it. The words take us by the hand and lead us from a romantic story to an understanding of how ordinary characters became caught up in a larger story. It says in effect, 'See now how God has woven the things that happened to these characters into the story He is telling – the story of salvation. Ruth became the mother of Obed, who was the father of Jesse, who was the father of David ... from whose line the Messiah Himself was born.'

The story of Ruth, therefore, though a narrative in its own right, must not be read in isolation. It is a story which leads us into God's epic. And anyone can get into that story – providing they are willing to come in through the door, which is, of course, Jesus Christ.

FURTHER STUDY

Acts 2:36-41;
Rom. 10:4-17

1. What did Peter proclaim?

2. What did Paul explain?

O Father, how can I ever thank You enough that I have entered through the door and become part of Your salvation story? Anything that happens to me is bearable when I see it as contributing to Your story. Amen.

God's great redemptive range

FOR READING & MEDITATION – RUTH 4:18-22

'... Boaz the father of Obed, Obed the father of Jesse,
and Jesse the father of David.' (vv.21-22)

Genealogies in the Bible are regarded by many as rather uninteresting and seemingly irrelevant, but the information they provide reveals some of the most exciting aspects of God's story. We saw yesterday how the simple statement: 'And they named him Obed. He was the father of Jesse, the father of David' (4:17), tells us that Ruth was the great-grandmother of King David, from whose line came our Lord Jesus Christ.

Matthew 1, which we looked at earlier in our studies and which provides the genealogy of Jesus, has a connection with the thoughts that have been occupying us as it mentions the name of Ruth. In fact, Matthew's genealogy is highly unusual because it departs from the normal custom of listing the male line only and includes the names of four women: Tamar, Rahab, Ruth, and Solomon's mother, Bathsheba. Tamar tricked her father-in-law into fathering her child (Gen. 38:18). Rahab was a prostitute who lived in Jericho (Josh. 2). Ruth, as we have seen, is referred to several times as a Moabitess – a foreigner. Bathsheba was the wife of Uriah the Hittite, and had an adulterous affair with King David (2 Sam.11:4). Commentators have pointed out that each of these women was either foreign, immoral or undesirable, and yet was included in the Messianic family tree.

FURTHER STUDY

Acts 11:1-18

1. Why was Peter criticised?

2. What was his defence?

This is what Eugene Peterson says concerning this point: 'Redemptive history is inventive and incorporative. It doesn't make any difference who your mother was. Anyone can get into the family. Anyone's personal history can be incorporated into the family history.' Though at first glance genealogical lists may seem tedious, the reality is that they demonstrate most powerfully God's redemptive ways.

Father, I am awestruck when I think about the endless ways You have of redeeming situations. Your skill at turning negatives into positives not only fascinates me but encourages me. Thank You Father. Amen.

FOR READING & MEDITATION – REVELATION 2:12–17

'I will also give him a white stone with a new name written on it,
known only to him who receives it.' (v.17)

Yesterday we saw that the genealogical lists in the Bible, synonymous in so many minds with monotony and irrelevance, become, when we understand their purpose, some of the most exciting parts of Scripture. It has not escaped your attention, I am sure, that there are few nameless people in the Bible. Scripture, as someone has put it, is 'thick with names'. 'The name,' says one writer, 'is the form of speech by which a person is singled out for personal love, particular intimacy, and exact responsibilities.'

That great storyteller of Victorian times, George MacDonald, knew how important a name is. In his exposition of the text before us today he wrote, 'The giving of the white stone with the new name is the communication of what God thinks about the man to the man. The true name is one which expressed the character, the nature, the meaning of the person who bears it ... Who can give a man this, his own name? God alone. For no one but God sees what the man is ... It is only when the man has become his name that God gives him the stone with his name upon it, for then first can he understand what his name signifies.' One day every believer is going to have a new name – a name that perfectly describes the person to whom it has been given.

FURTHER STUDY

Gen. 25:24–26;
32:24–28;
Acts 11:19–26

1. Why was Jacob's name changed?

2. What was special about the Antioch Christians?

What does all this say to us? It says this: God's love extends to details and is a love that delights to minister to us not just corporately but individually. If you find it hard to believe that you will be of consequence in heaven because you feel you are of such little consequence down here on earth then think about this: God has reserved for you a new name which will be given to you because of what you have become.

O Father, the more I see how Your love extends to details, the more my love flows out towards You. I can't wait to receive my new name describing the character You have formed in me. Thank You my Father. Amen.

Christ - God's alphabet

FOR READING & MEDITATION - REVELATION 1:1-8

'"I am the Alpha and the Omega," says the Lord God ...' (v.8)

Before we leave the story of Ruth and move on to other aspects of our theme we pause to make this central point once again: lovely as the story of Ruth is, it is not the whole story. The whole story is about the Messiah – the One whom our text for today describes as the 'Alpha and Omega'. Alpha and Omega, as many of you will know, are the first and last letters of the Greek alphabet, and the term 'Alpha and Omega' is used to signify the beginning and the end.

Some time ago I came across this by an anonymous writer: 'Christ is the alphabet out of which God frames every sentence, every paragraph, and every chapter of His salvation story.' When I first read that I remember shouting to myself *He is!* As we acknowledged earlier, every road in the Old Testament converges on Him and every road in the New Testament emerges from Him. Everything in the Bible revolves around Jesus Christ. Little did the women who prayed that Ruth would be 'like Rachel and Leah' (Ruth 4:11) know that the small town of Bethlehem would be set in the mainstream of God's wonderful purposes and become the birthplace of the Saviour Himself. It was one of the roads that led to *Him*.

The story recorded in the book of Ruth leads us ultimately to Jesus Christ. Though Ruth, Naomi and Boaz were the participants, it is because of their relationship to Jesus Christ that they take on their significance. And it is the same with you and me. Our life stories may in themselves be interesting, even absorbing, but what makes them *significant* is when, through our relationship with Jesus Christ, they are woven into *His* story. Our names are on Christ's family tree – not prior to His coming, of course, but subsequent to it.

FURTHER STUDY

Acts 4:13-22;
Eph. 1:11-14;
2:11-13

1. What made ordinary fishermen significant?

2. What makes excluded Gentiles significant?

Father, I bow before You once again with gratitude in my heart that through Your Son's sacrifice for me on the cross I, an outsider, am now an insider. My name is on the Saviour's family tree. Hallelujah!

Accepting the inevitable

FOR READING & MEDITATION – PSALM 73:1-28
'Surely in vain have I kept my heart pure ...' (v.13)

Having seen something of the way in which God weaves the details of our lives into His big story we move on now to consider the question: How should we live as participants in God's big story? First, we must accept the inevitabilities of life. A famous psychiatrist, M. Scott-Peck, to whom I have often referred in the past, began his book *The Road Less Travelled* with these words: 'Life is difficult.' Once we face that fact, he points out, 'once we truly know that life is difficult, then life is no longer difficult. Because once it is accepted, the fact that life is difficult no longer matters. Then we can transcend it.'

We have been born into a fallen world, and things inevitably happen that are not to our liking. As Christians we must not expect to be exempted from the consequences of the Fall. It is true that sometimes God overcomes its effects (when, for instance, He mercifully heals our illnesses). But even those who have experienced His healing touch (and I am one of them) know that God does not heal every illness and that eventually every one of us will have to die.

Some Christians still claim that if we live close to Jesus Christ then it is possible to live a life that is free from all troubles and illness – a kind of Garden of Eden experience. But there is no way back into the Garden of Eden because God positioned some angelic bouncers there (Gen. 3:24). Something better than the Garden of Eden awaits us, but it lies up ahead. Meanwhile we wait, and accept life's inevitabilities with fortitude and grace. 'Here,' as a friend of mine puts it, 'there is something wrong with everything; there [speaking of heaven] nothing will be wrong with anything.'

FURTHER STUDY

Rom. 8:18-25; 2 Cor. 12:7-10

1. What has Christ's sacrifice not done in the present?

2. Why can we delight in troubles?

My Father and my God, help me to understand that I live in a fallen world, and that though evil and disease are not part of Your good purposes, I have to live with them. Teach me how to accept the things I cannot change. In Jesus' name. Amen.

Don't dam the stream

FOR READING & MEDITATION - JOB 21:1-21

'Who is the Almighty, that we should serve him?' (v.15)

Yesterday we said that the first thing we must do in living as a participant in God's big story is to accept the inevitable. If we insist that because we are Christians we should be exempt from the effects of the Fall, our attitude will bring us into conflict with God's purposes for our lives. We can accept whatever happens to us with grace and not with a grudge. God is unable to work the divine alchemy in a heart that harbours resentment.

Take, for instance, the matter of bereavement. Some people suffer a crushing loss but never come to terms with it in their hearts. They accept that they cannot summon the one they loved from the dead, but they still remain bitter. They envy the happiness of others and resent the good health that those whom they regard as undeserving appear to enjoy. In their hearts they are hostile to God. Similarly Job, as we see from the passage we have read today, experienced some moments of antagonism towards God. Later on, however, he came to see the foolishness of his position.

FURTHER STUDY

Mark 6:17-29;
Heb. 12:14-15

1. How may we nurse a grudge like Herodias?

2. What is the antidote to grudges?

Dr Barnardo, the founder of Barnado's children's homes in Britain, lost his little son from diphtheria when he was nine years of age. Did he accuse heaven of being unfair, and protest to the Almighty? No. He said, 'As my dear little boy lay gasping in my arms and as I gazed into the little pinched face growing cold in death, hundreds of other children's faces appeared to me through his. I resolved afresh that by God's grace I would consecrate myself anew to the blessed task of rescuing helpless little ones from the miseries of a neglected and sinful life.'

Are you harbouring a grudge? Dare to surrender it now. Grace may flow like a river but a grudge will dam the stream.

O God, forgive me if a grudge is damming the stream of Your grace. Help me surrender all my grudges to You right now so that grace might flow uninterrupted through my heart. In Christ's name I pray. Amen.

The power of lament

FOR READING & MEDITATION – PSALM 55:1-23

'My heart is in anguish within me; the terrors of death assail me.' (v.4)

Another matter we need to face as participants in God's big story is this: we must be willing to lament. I am aware that this theme is not popular with the majority of Christians today, who seem to think that when a negative feeling arises, it is best to pretend it isn't there. Do you realise that 70 per cent of the psalms are laments? These laments arose from the disappointments, losses and tragedies the psalmists faced, because they did not avoid these issues or deny that things were as they were.

One commentator says, 'The theology of lament is one of the most under-emphasised aspects of today's Christian culture.'

Eugene Peterson, when contrasting the psalms with the secular culture of our day, said, 'We have a style of print and media journalism that reports disaster endlessly. In the wake of whatever has gone wrong or whatever wrong is done, commentators gossip, reporters interview, editors pontificate, pharisees moralise, but there is not one line of lament.' Notice these words: *there is not one line of lament.* Few of today's secular writers are ready to mourn the violation of moral principles. And why? Because generally speaking such things as truth, righteousness and love are not taken seriously in today's world. What counts is 'news'. People cry out for the facts, and often are not interested in the underlying ethical issues. I tell you, when we trivialise the virtues of truth, righteousness and love, then our culture is heading for the rocks.

Look again at David's words in Psalm 55. He faces everything, and prays through everything. Eugene Peterson claims that 'the craggy majesty and towering dignity of David's life are a product of David's laments'. I agree.

My Father and my God, help me understand the importance of lament. Save me from trying to get from one place to another too quickly, without giving my soul time to feel the pain. In Jesus' name I pray. Amen.

'The angry psalms'

FOR READING & MEDITATION - PSALM 64:1-10
'Hear me, O God, as I voice my complaint ...' (v.1)

Yesterday we noted that the majority of the psalms are laments. One Christian said in connection with the psalms of lament, 'I never read the angry psalms as they make it harder, not easier, for me to trust in God. I feel when I read them that I am doing little more than grumbling against God – something the Bible condemns.'

Dan Allender makes this point: 'Lament is as different from grumbling as a search is from aimless wandering.' A grumbler has already reached a conclusion about life, has shut down all open-mindedness with questions that are barely concealed accusations. In contrast, a person uttering a lament is expressing a desire to understand what is happening. That person is knocking at the door of God's heart and saying, 'Help me comprehend what is going on, what is the purpose behind my predicament.' He or she is not ranting and raving with conclusions they have already reached, but pouring out painful feelings in the hope that some answers might be given. Lament is a cry of agony.

Psalm 80 has several examples. Here is just one of them: 'O LORD God Almighty, how long will your anger smoulder against the prayers of your people?' (v.4). Lament, properly understood, is entering the agony of loss, an expression of a desire for understanding.

Notice how often the psalmists, after they have expressed their pain, fall back into the arms of God and say, 'But as for me, I trust in you' (Psa. 55:23). When you lament you are being real with your emotions, being true to how you feel about what has happened to you. But having expressed your feelings, you then fall back on the certainty that God knows exactly what He is doing. There is a place for lament in the lives of all of us and it has great power.

FURTHER STUDY

Psa. 42:1-43:5

1. How was the psalmist real with his emotions?

2. What was the fall-back position?

Teach me the power of lament, my Father, so that I might deal with all my soul's needs in a way that contributes to my spiritual health. Save me, I pray, from the kind of idealism that has no realism. In Jesus' name. Amen.

Knowing God better

FOR READING & MEDITATION – PSALM 77:1-20
'When I was in distress, I sought the Lord ...' (v.2)

We must spend another day reflecting on the significance of lament. The reason why the psalms of lament are included in Scripture is because we need to see the importance of being honest and real about our emotions. When loss strikes us or dampening disappointments affect our lives, we must be willing to face the pain and feel it. It is not easy, as a certain Christian once told me, to come to terms with some personal tragedy when you have just read words like these: 'A thousand may fall at your side, ten thousand at your right hand, but it will not come near you' (Psa. 91:7). We struggle at such times, and lament is part of that struggle.

FURTHER STUDY

Lam. 3:19-26;
Mark 14:32-42

1. What did Jeremiah call to mind in the midst of lament?

2. How did a period of lament affect Jesus?

Lament has the potential to change our attitudes because it compels us to strip our hearts of all pretence and forces us to wrestle with God. And out of that wrestling will come a new awareness of God and a new sense of His presence. There is no guarantee that our questions will be answered, but we will know *Him* better.

Many who study the psalms wonder why, as in the psalm before us, one moment the writer can seemingly rail against God, and then the next moment affirm His goodness. This is simply the experience of the soul rising through confusion – even anger – to recognise that, after all, God knows what He is doing and that He is good. And the struggles we go through to reach that conclusion are in themselves strengthening. Lament has been described as making the most of our losses and disappointments without getting bogged down in them. We admit how we are feeling, struggle with it, and then move on to acknowledge the greatness and goodness of our God. Lament is an important way of participating in God's story.

O Father, I see that if I want to be involved in Your story then dealing honestly with the affairs of my soul is part of that process. Lament is a sober subject but a necessary one. Please help me as I seek to understand it more thoroughly. Amen.

How evil can become good

FOR READING & MEDITATION - PSALM 9:1-10
'I will be glad and rejoice in you ...' (v.2)

Over the past few days we have been saying that to be a participant in God's big story we must be willing to give up our grudges, accept the inevitable, and be ready to lament. But another point is this: we must believe in God's power to change things. Unbelief can hinder (though not outmanoeuvre) even the Almighty. So develop confidence in God's skill at turning life's setbacks into springboards. He can take even the most evil situation and make it work for good.

A curious thing happened in South Africa some years ago. A black woman was found guilty of a minor offence and fined a sum that amounted to the value of a gold coin she had in her possession, which had been bequeathed to her by her mother. When she handed the coin to the clerk of the court, he saw that according to the current gold standard, the coin was now worth much more than its face value. So he gave back to her in change a sum that exceeded what she thought the coin was worth. Knowing nothing about the gold standard, the woman left the court with her mind in a whirl. Back home in her village she asked her friends how she could possibly be condemned for a crime and yet be paid a dividend.

FURTHER STUDY

Dan. 3:13-30;
Acts 8:1-8

1. What good resulted from the king's evil act?

2. What was the result of persecution?

You may have experienced something similar in a different realm of life. Evil is evil, you say, tragedy is tragedy. Nothing can alter that. The death of someone you loved, the loss of an investment, a spouse's infidelity, hateful slander – these are things fit only for condemnation. How can one gain by them? The answer is: accept what happens without bitterness, enter into it with lament for an appropriate length of time, and have faith in God's transforming power. You will find that He can bring good out of everything bad.

Father, I might not live to see some of the transformations You are bringing about, but those who come after me may exclaim with the psalmist, 'The Lord has done this, and it is marvellous in our eyes.' For that I am thankful. Amen.

When sin recoiled

FOR READING & MEDITATION – COLOSSIANS 2:6-15

'And having disarmed the powers ... he made a public spectacle of them, triumphing over them by the cross.' (v.15)

Yesterday we said that God can transform everything that happens and make it work for good – even the worst form of evil. Think of the cross. That is the supreme example. If God could transform what happened there, He can do the same anywhere. At the cross, He took the foulest thing that has ever occurred and made it into the most sublime. The crucifixion is the world's worst sin; it is the world's supreme hope. It is the very essence of evil; it is the highest expression of love.

One writer has said this: "If a friend or a member of your family had died on a gallows you would not walk about with a gold gibbet around your neck. You would seek to hide his shame from every eye. But the manner of Christ's dying we hold up to all the world. The top of a church steeple is not too high for it; the communion table is barely prominent enough. Observe how complete is the transformation. It is His message it bears, not that of the ones who crucified Him.' When the sound of the last hammer stroke fell on the ears of the crowd and the cross was dropped into its socket they might have expected curses, but instead they heard Jesus say, 'Father, forgive them, for they do not know what they are doing' (Luke 23:34). The mystic alchemy had begun. Sin recoiled, was beaten, and became only the dark background of His radiant love.

FURTHER STUDY

John 12:23-33;
Rom. 8:28-34

1. How did Jesus explain?

2. What did Paul affirm?

If God can do that with the cross what might He not do with the evil that comes into our lives? Will He be beaten by abuse, rampant hatred, crime, loss? No. He will dip His pen in these dark colours and write a story that will transform the evil into good. *God* is telling this story, remember – the greatest story writer in all the universe.

O Father, whenever doubts assail me about Your ability to turn evil to good, help me linger at the cross. There the worst thing that could ever have happened was turned into the best thing that could ever happen. Glory be to Your name. Amen.

Entering into mystery

FOR READING & MEDITATION - JOB 42:1-6

'Surely I spoke of things I did not understand, things too wonderful for me to know.' (v.3)

Another thing we must do as participants in God's big story is to enter into mystery and celebrate it. (This is a matter we thought about earlier this year in the January/February issue of *Every Day with Jesus, The Nature of the Spiritual Journey*.) What do I mean when I say we must enter into mystery? Let me put it like this: most of us, when we are faced with mystery, instead of entering into it and rejoicing that God knows more than we do, attempt to resolve the mystery by reducing it to manageable proportions. Mystery erodes our sense of competence so we struggle to explain it, to rationalise it.

Some of God's 'mysterious' purposes, of course, can be explained. The romantic purpose that we talked about earlier is something that, once explained, can easily be comprehended. However, some things that happen to us cannot be understood, no matter how hard we try to make sense of them, for we are, as C.S. Lewis said, riding 'with our backs to the engine'. We are not able to see what the train driver can see up ahead. So we must enter into the mysteries and celebrate them, trusting that our lives are in safe hands. Mystery challenges us in the area of trust. God allows things to happen to us that have no apparent explanation, and so we accept and deal with whatever God is doing with absolute trust.

FURTHER STUDY

Psa. 139:1-12;
Isa. 40:21-31

1. What could the psalmist not attain?

2. What did Isaiah understand he could not understand?

In one of his stories C.S. Lewis talks about a girl named Lucy who asks one of the other characters, Mr Beaver, about Aslan the Lion (a symbol of Christ): 'Is he safe?' 'No,' says Mr Beaver, 'he is not safe, but he is good.' The world in which we live is not safe, but God is good. We must go on believing that even in the presence of the deepest of mysteries.

My Father and my God, take my hand and walk with me through every mysterious situation in which I find myself. And help me remember that though sometimes life may be bad, You are always good. In Jesus' name. Amen.

Rejoice in mystery

FOR READING & MEDITATION - PSALM 45:1-17

'My heart is stirred by a noble theme as I recite my verses
for the king ...' (v.1)

You may remember that when we were talking about Naomi's role, I said God did not delete the complaint she made about her situation from the inspired record but kept it and used it to advance His purposes. This statement, which I came across some time ago, intrigued me: 'God does not look kindly on our editorial deletions, but He delights in our poetry.' What does that mean, I wondered.

As I thought about it, this was my conclusion. There is a difference between poetry and prose. In nature and purpose they are totally distinct. Poetry is the product of passion. It has something volcanic about it, surging up in the poet's soul like molten lava and spilling over in strangely moving language. The poet cannot help but write a poem. He or she writes it even if nobody is ever likely to read it. In fact, some poets are not too concerned if no one does read their poems; all they want to do is to give their thoughts verbal expression. Not so prose. Speaking generally, a prose writer first makes up his mind what he wants to say and then says it as plainly as possible.

FURTHER STUDY

Psa. 71:14-24;
Phil. 4:4

1. Why would the psalmist praise more and more?

2. What did Paul emphasise?

When the author of the statement quoted above talks about God not looking kindly on our editorial deletions but delighting in our poetry, I believe he is thinking of the different approaches that a poet and a prose writer might have to the mysterious. The prose writer might look at things analytically and say, 'I need more illumination before I can comment.' The poet is more likely to respond by entering into the mystery and composing a poem about it. This is what the psalmist is doing in the psalm we have read today. He doesn't attempt to manage the mystery of God; he simply rejoices in it.

O Father, grant that I may respond to what You are doing in my life with the poetry of thanksgiving and praise. Save me from seeking to make editorial deletions. Instead, may I receive everything with grace and gratitude. Amen.

To know God is the greatest goal a man or woman can have. And God wants to be known. He longs to be intimately involved in the lives of each one of us.

In the next issue of *Every Day with Jesus*, Selwyn leads us through the Old Testament, looking at the names God used to reveal Himself to His people. A name, when used in the Bible, is not merely a designation; it is a definition. The names of God reveal characteristics about Him which, when we reflect on them, can have a bearing on our own lives and character.

Ultimately, however, God has revealed Himself through His Son, who is called Jesus – 'Jehovah saves'. Through Him we can be adopted into God's family and change our own names – we become known as children of God.

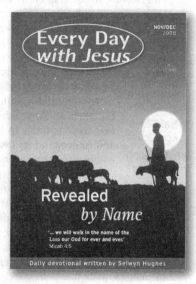

Every Day
with Jesus

NOV/DEC
2008

Revealed
by Name

'... we will walk in the name of the LORD our God for ever and ever.'
Micah 4:5

Daily devotional written by Selwyn Hughes

More about poetry

FOR READING & MEDITATION – ROMANS 11:25-36

'Oh, the depth of the riches of ... God! How unsearchable his judgments, and his paths beyond tracing out!' (v.33)

We continue thinking about the statement we looked at yesterday: 'God does not look kindly on our editorial deletions, but He delights in our poetry.' G.K. Chesterton, in his book *The Romance of Faith*, said that when you face life honestly you become aware that chess players go mad but poets never do. He is using an hyperbole, of course – exaggeration for the sake of emphasis. A chess player is constantly working on strategy, and tries to find some order in an attempt to understand things. Once, when I was watching my favourite television programme, *Star Trek: The Next Generation*, I heard Commander Data, the Android,

FURTHER STUDY

Psa. 92:1-5;
Eccl. 3:1-14

1. What is good for us?

2. What did Solomon realise?

say that he preferred chess to poetry because he was more comfortable with order that could be manipulated. But then an Android has no emotion. A poet realises that there is order in life but he doesn't struggle to try and understand it; instead he floats on the waves and enters into the mystery of it through poetry.

When faced with the mystery of God's story in our lives we have two choices: either we respond by trying to figure out God's ways and seek to introduce some 'editorial deletions', or we respond by floating on the waves of His purposes and say, 'Lord, I praise You because Your ways are beyond tracing out', as Paul does in the passage we have just read. Poets recognise mystery and rejoice in it without trying to manage it.

Don't try to make sense of mystery when you find yourself caught up in it. Respond poetically to it. Rejoice in it. The very nature of existence requires that we be poets and not chess players. Blessed are those who allow themselves to be awed by what God is doing in their lives and respond to it with poetic rhythm and praise.

Father, help me respond to life's mysteries in the same way that Paul did – not by attempting to figure things out but by bowing in wonder, love and praise. Amen.

Don't sigh - sing!

FOR READING & MEDITATION - 1 SAMUEL 1:21-2:11

'As surely as you live, my lord, I am the woman who stood here beside you praying to the LORD.' (1:26)

Surely there can be no greater thrill than knowing that we are caught up in God's big story. Take the case of Hannah. You are probably familiar with the story, but permit me to briefly sketch some of the details.

Hannah was one of Elkanah's two wives, the other being Peninnah. Peninnah, we read, 'had children, but Hannah had none' (1:2). Regularly, Peninnah would scorn Hannah and make fun of her because she was infertile (1:6-7). But though deeply hurt, Hannah appears to have handled the situation with dignity and restraint. In the Temple Hannah pours out her soul to the Lord (1:15), and God hears her prayer. She conceives and gives birth to a child whom she names Samuel. A little while after his birth, Hannah keeps the promise she has made and presents Samuel to the Lord for a lifetime of service in the Temple. As she hands Samuel over to the Lord, she sings a song that is one of the most beautiful in Scripture. But notice *when* she sang her song – not when Samuel was conceived or born, but when she gave him up to the service of the Lord.

FURTHER STUDY

2 Chron. 20:1-24

1. Who led the army?

2. When did the Lord bring deliverance?

Dr Larry Crabb says, 'The deepest and richest songs are sung, not in the moments of blessing, but in those moments when we sense we are being caught up in the movement of God, that we have been lifted into a larger story.' Mary, the mother of Jesus, sang her most sublime song when she realised she was being caught up in a divine movement that would bring salvation to the world (Luke 1:46-55). Are you aware at the moment of something going on in your life that is bigger than your personal agenda – that you are being caught up in a bigger story? Then sing your song! It will be the most significant song you will ever sing.

My Father and my God, whenever I feel called to give something up – to surrender it to You – help me see my action in the context of the bigger story. And instead of sighing help me sing. In Jesus' name. Amen.

A transcendent drama

FOR READING & MEDITATION – ISAIAH 38:9-22

'Surely it was for my benefit that I suffered such anguish.' (v.17)

A good part of my life has been spent listening to people's stories. I have discovered that people can tell their story in many different ways. Some tell it as if it is a comedy – they joke about it because to deal with it seriously would reduce them to tears. Others tell it as a tragedy – they see no point in what has happened to them. Then there are those who tell it as an irony – they speak mockingly about the fitness of things. But I have met some – all too few – who talk about their lives in terms of a transcendent drama. They recount the things that have happened to them with the clear awareness that a loving God has allowed them to pass through these things for a purpose.

Whenever I have listened to Joni Eareckson Tada tell her story, for example, I hear nothing that comes anywhere close to tragedy, comedy or irony. There is something inspiring, something of God, about her story. She talks about the events that made her a quadriplegic not in terms of tragedy but in terms of a transcendent drama. One has only to listen to her to be aware of the grace of God that shines out from her personality. She has the attention and admiration of millions because she speaks out of suffering – suffering that has been redeemed. She admits, of course, that there was a time of complaint in her life – a time when she shook her fist in God's face – but she has worked through that now and has come to recognise that in allowing her accident to take place, God had a purpose for her life that has touched the lives of millions.

How would you tell the story of your life if you were asked, I wonder? As a comedy, a tragedy, an irony, or a transcendent drama?

Father, I am on the spot. How would I tell my story? As a comedy, a tragedy, an irony or a divine drama? Please help me think this matter through today. In Christ's name I pray. Amen.

How do I get in?

FOR READING & MEDITATION - JOHN 3:1-15

'I tell you the truth, no-one can see the kingdom of God unless he is born again.' (v.3)

One thing I feel I must do as we draw to a close is to invite those who do not know Jesus Christ to become part of His story. In many areas of the world *Every Day with Jesus* is read by people who are interested in Christian things but have not yet committed themselves to Jesus. Today I want to invite those of you who are not yet included in God's salvation story to enter into it. And so, for the benefit of those who do not know Him personally, I pose this question: How do I enter into a relationship with God and become part of His eternal epic?

You enter into a personal relationship with God through His Son Jesus by being what the Bible calls 'born again'. I once preached a series of sermons on the text 'You must be born again' (v.7), which were spread over six Sunday evenings. Someone asked me why I took the same text six successive Sunday evenings. I replied, 'Because you must be born again.' The necessity of the new birth is spoken of throughout the New Testament. We divide people into races, sexes, nationalities, the rich and the poor, the educated and the uneducated, but Jesus divided all men and women into only two classes: the once born and the twice born.

FURTHER STUDY

John 1:1-13; 3:16-18

1. What is the difference between physical and spiritual birth?

2. Why did God send Jesus?

If you already know Jesus Christ, if you have been born again, you are in the kingdom of God, and if you are not, then you are not in His kingdom. If you have not been born again I invite you now to open your heart to God and His Son Jesus Christ. Say the following prayer and you will receive the new birth as countless multitudes down the ages have done. You will be born again.

Heavenly Father, I want to be part of Your story. I come to You now to be born again. I surrender everything to You - my whole life, my heart ... everything. Accept me and make me Your child. In Jesus' name I pray.

'In my own voice'

FOR READING & MEDITATION - COLOSSIANS 1:1-14
'We are asking God that you may see things, as it were, from his point of view ...' (v.9, Phillips)

On this our last day of thinking together about God as the divine story writer I would like to drop into your heart this thought: no matter how insignificant you may feel, if you believe in the Lord Jesus Christ and have been born again, the truth is that you are included in God's big story. Your name is written into His universal epic. One day, when the whole story is unfolded in eternity, you will see what part you have played in the eternal scheme of things. You don't have to spend your time scrupulously trying to figure out in what scene you appear. Trust that the Casting Director has given you a role that highlights not only your special talents and individuality but, more importantly, the way in which divine grace is at work in your life.

FURTHER STUDY

Rom. 12:1-13;
Col. 4:5-6;
1 Pet. 3:15

1. What did Paul teach?

2. What do both Paul and Peter tell us to do?

Just to be part of God's great epic, to be caught up in the narrative He is telling, is one of the highest privileges afforded any human being. A friend of mine, Phil Greenslade, says, 'I don't mind being just a spear carrier as long as I am part of God's big story.'

I leave you with these lines by Paul Goodman, which he describes as 'a little prayer':

Page after page I have lived Your world
In the narrative manner, Lord,
In my own voice I tell Your story.

In my own voice I tell *Your story.* Powerful words. How different life is when we realise that through all that happens to us a divine story, a bigger story, is being written. Drop your anchor into the depths of this reassuring and encouraging revelation. In the strongest currents of life it will, I promise, help to hold you fast.

My Father and my God, how can I ever sufficiently thank You for the priceless privilege of telling in my own voice Your story? Help me from this day forward to see all things from Your point of view. In Jesus' name. Amen.